The Subtle Shark:
Redefining Career Achievement

By

Ayesha R. Patterson

ISBN:0989624404
ISBN-13:978-0-9896244-0-4

Cover Design by:
Warren Polk III

Edited by :
In The Words Consulting

Photographer:
© Jennifer Orr

DEDICATION

I dedicate this book to my biggest cheerleaders, Diane & Daddy. They never hesitate to tell me how proud they are, which inspires me to keep going. They provide the moral compass that keeps me headed in the right direction. Their love and excitement is contagious and fuels my spirit.

CONTENTS

ACKNOWLEDGMENTS

I am profoundly grateful and blessed to have such a strong and deep support system. My extended family is far too large to mention everyone by name. I just hope that I express through my actions how appreciative I am to be loved by them.

Special thanks to Bridgette Outten for coming up with the book's title when I was struggling to think of something "catchy".

My entire Great Lakes Repair team may all be split up now, but it was a pleasure to serve them to the best of my abilities.

Thanks to Team 610 for helping me with my professional growth. We went through a lot together. It was one heck of a ride.

I already know it won't be enough for me to have written about my sister, Cherry in the book. So I'll acknowledge her here too.

Thanks to my favorite "BEAR" for providing me safety, friendship, partnership and laughter.

Lastly, thanks to my favorite ANGELS, Grandma, Gramps, Wallace & Mama Phyllis as they watch over me in spirit.

INTRODUCTION

As I write this book, I am at the beginning of a journey in my second career as a business consultant and coach. Launching my own company took a huge leap of faith. I come from a family of self-starters and entrepreneurs, which gave me the confidence and ambition I needed to take on such a challenge. I have worked a few different jobs up to this point and with each I was able to learn something that made me more successful in the next. It all culminated in my longest running job to date, working for Best Buy. I spent over 19 years at the company, beginning as a part-time cashier and ending as a Service Repair General Manager (a title that just does not capture the magnitude of the job itself). By the time I left, I was responsible for almost 400 employees throughout 13 states.

I am extremely proud of my accomplishments because it took a lot of determination and focus to achieve them. I am even more proud that I did not have to compromise my beliefs and who I am as a person. Throughout my career, I saw so many people who "sold their soul" to get promotions and became "drunk" with their perceived power. Some may assume that in order to move up in the business world one has to be cold and conniving. Newsflash: I did pretty well without going about it that way.

So, I wrote this book to share who I am, how I became the person I am, and how I achieved some pretty lofty career goals without changing fundamentally. You may see pieces of yourself and your situation in some of my stories and experiences. As you read *The Subtle Shark*, you will notice that I have included some of my personal journal entries. I've kept a diary since high school and once I narrowed down my career path, my on-the-job occurrences became the focus of many writings. You will see my mindset at particular points in time, my professional growth and maturity first hand. I hope that you enjoy the expedition and glean from it some insight and motivation. The Subtle Shark Traits worksheet in the Appendix is meant to help you in your journey.

Many myths about sharks paint them as dimwitted, wild creatures that hunt for sport. And though they are dangerous, their survival techniques are often misunderstood. Throughout my career I have been able to endure and thrive with the edge of a shark, but with a more delicate touch. Sometimes it has taken a while for others to recognize my capabilities because I crept in under their radar, like a subtle shark. I hope this book serves as an inspiration for those who think they have to be uber-educated, extraordinarily charismatic or annoyingly aggressive to get ahead. I am none of those things and I was able to do it.

CHAPTER ONE
HABITAT

Shark pups are not cared for by their mothers when born. They come into the world ready to hunt, with natural survival instincts and a full set of teeth. Unlike a baby shark, I did grow up with the protection and guidance of my family, but I displayed the ability to look after myself early in life.

On my first day of kindergarten, the teacher told my mother that we would be dismissed an hour later than school actually let out. I stood and waited in the spot where my mother was to pick me up for about 30 minutes.   By that time, no one was around because all the other children had been retrieved. Although I was instructed by my mother to wait until she got there, I felt like it was dangerous to be alone. Besides, I was pretty sure I knew how to get home, so I started walking. Admittedly, I was frightened and crying, but that wasn't going to stop me from getting to safety. Just as I walked up to our house, my mother and sister were leaving to come get me. Words can't express how happy I was to see them. But I was proud that I had made it home on my own!

Though that incident showcased my survival behavior, it did not negate the need for the direction, nurturing and shelter that my family created in our habitat. There is no doubt that many of my Subtle Shark traits come from my family of sharks, each with their own characteristics.

THE RESPONSIBLE SHARK

I am going to start with my mother, Diane. My sister and I have never called her anything other than Diane or Di... at her request. She does not believe in "titles," and insists that everyone calls her by her first name. Understandably, people are usually shocked when I share that bit of information, but it is not a big deal to me because that's how it's always been. As far as I'm concerned, Diane equals Mom.

Diane has always taken her job as a mother very seriously. Her goal was to make sure we had a healthy self-esteem and were productive members of society.

With this in mind, Diane had my sister and me working from very young ages.

We started washing dishes when I was eight-years-old and my sister was six. Di says we broke plenty of dishes at that time, but we learned. Two years prior I was making my own breakfast. Granted, it was just instant oatmeal and my mother boiled the water for me, but I opened the packet myself and stirred in the water. I consider that *making* breakfast. By the time my sister and I were eight and ten, respectively, we were vacuuming, dusting and a little bit of cooking.

I am a very process-driven person, and it's no doubt that I get it from Diane. Working with her in the sewing room and boutique, I learned the importance of keeping detailed records and being efficient. As a designer and seamstress, Diane ran a small business out of our home for several years while working a full-time job. One of my first assignments was picking up stick pins from the floor in her sewing room. I'm pretty sure I didn't get paid any money, but there was always some kind of treat as compensation. For a couple of months we did have a job shredding papers at the hospital where she worked as the Payroll Supervisor. We actually received a paycheck for that job. As we got older, Diane would give us more sewing room responsibilities like ironing seams, hems and pockets, cutting patterns, running elastic among other things. By the time I graduated from high school, we were working part-time hours in the sewing room and boutique. We had scheduled work hours and break times. We assisted with inventory tracking, prepping for fashion shows and helping customers. Though there was still no paycheck, we did get extra money for school events and activities. As a seamstress Diane was very detailed and made sure she produced a quality product. That focus was evident in every aspect of the business. Diane always had processes in place for everything that needed to be done. She was very meticulous about assigning inventory numbers to every garment and tracking her production. I picked up on all of that. In fact, I am very uncomfortable and unable to move forward if there is no process in place when I am working.

Another important quality I learned from Diane was integrity.

As a child, I would take things that didn't belong to me, and when I got caught (which was always), I'd lie about it. Well, Diane wasn't having it. I remember when I was about eight or nine-years-old I swiped something off of Di's dresser and got busted. I don't recall what the item was, but it was the straw that broke the camel's back. I didn't get a regular spanking, whooping, or whatever you want to call it. I got a straight up beat down! Needless to say, that was the last time I stole anything. Diane always told us that she adopted her father's philosophy of not tolerating thieves and liars. She wanted to make sure she broke me of that bad habit very quickly before I got out into the world and it turned into a career. It took me a little longer to stop lying, but she always reminded us that "your word is your bond" and without it, you have nothing.

THE SUBTLE SHARK IS TRUSTWORTHY

★ ★ ★ ★ ★ ★ ★ ★ ★ ★ ★ ★

Subtle Shark Exploration

In your career or your business, how do you build trust with others?

What personal values guide your professional interactions?

★ ★ ★ ★ ★ ★ ★ ★ ★ ★ ★ ★

As with most mothers and daughters, we had our conflicts, especially when I was in my early twenties. I had veered off course, made some poor choices and Diane was upset about it. But the more she wanted to address things and get to what she considered to be the root cause(s) of my behavior, the more I wanted to shut down.

Journal Entry 3/26/95- She is always digging for a deeper meaning for EVERYTHING and I'm beginning to think that it just doesn't work for all situations. She keeps trying to find out what was going on in my mind to make me defy her. All I can say is, she told me not to do something; I disagreed with it and did my own thing without considering the consequences. Nothing more, nothing less. I'm beginning to think that we'll never be able to relate.

Journal Entry 4/13/95- I've come to an understanding with my family that recent events and feelings have been a result of total misunderstandings. Hopefully some of Di's anger has subsided against me. We had a really long talk Tuesday and a lot of things got ironed out. I agreed to open up a little more and she agreed to compromise, even when she doesn't agree with me.

Once I started to display consistent responsible behavior, our relationship blossomed. I realized that being an adult is not about doing whatever I want, but what is right. Now we can talk about anything and respect each other's opinions.

THE ACHIEVEMENT SHARK

Mediocrity is not acceptable. That was one of the main values my father instilled in us early on. He said that it was our duty to always do our best and give 100% at all times. My father's name is Leland and in case you're wondering, we've always called him Daddy. Unlike Diane, he does believe in titles. He also believes in structure and discipline.

We used to get put on punishment if we earned C's on our report cards because he said that it was not good enough for me and my sister to be average. He felt that when we earned anything less than an A or a B, it was because we hadn't applied ourselves. And he was right. Usually if I ended up with a C in any subject it was because I didn't pay attention in class or didn't do the homework. I don't claim to be brilliant, but I have been blessed with the aptitude to get A's or B's without any extra studying, as long as I paid attention when the lesson was being taught.

THE SUBTLE SHARK DOES NOT ACCEPT MEDIOCRITY

★ ★ ★ ★ ★ ★ ★ ★ ★ ★ ★

Subtle Shark Exploration

In what ways do you strive for excellence in your career or business?

What personal characteristics of yourself and others do you consider "deal-breakers" in your professional dealings?

★ ★ ★ ★ ★ ★ ★ ★ ★ ★ ★

Growing up, my father had so many rules for us to follow. During meals we couldn't take a drink until we finished eating; we had to wear shoes at all times in the house; we had to wash dishes as soon as dinner was done and plenty of other things. I couldn't wait until I was old enough, so I could stop doing ALL of those things!

As stringent as the rules were, I know that they were for structure and our protection.

We were very obedient children because we knew that Daddy wasn't having anything less. Though we did our share of mischievous things, we weren't the type of kids that terrorized other patrons at restaurants, whined until we got what we wanted in the store or ran around the house tearing things up and making lots of noise. We usually only had to be warned once to cease and desist any inappropriate behavior. As a result, I have always conducted myself with poise and discipline.

Don't get me wrong, it wasn't all rules and regulations. I get my sense of adventure from my father. From a very young age, Daddy exposed us to so many fun things. He would take us with him when he went water skiing or to play sports. We'd take family trips to amusement parks and when I was old enough, he and I would ride every single roller coaster together; the bigger and faster, the better. He even had a motorcycle when I was really young and I remember he took me for a ride on it once. Daddy is always open to try new things and encouraged us to do the same. To this day, I'm still willing to jump out there and see where it leads me.

Dependability is another trait that I got from Daddy. Growing up and even now, I know that if I need something from my father, he will be there for me. If he said he was going to be at a certain place at a certain time to pick us up from an event, he was there early. When he says he is going to do something, you can rest assured that it will be done and done well.

Because I knew how good it felt to depend on my father, I've always strived to be as reliable with others because I want them to feel the same about me.

Probably most importantly, **I am influenced by Daddy's fortitude**. During my freshman year of high school he had brain surgery to remove his pituitary gland, which had grown into a tumor. As a result of the operation, his motor skills on the right side of his body had diminished. He was given a prognosis for how long it would take to fully recover, but he was resolute in cutting that time in half. When he got out of the hospital, my sister and I were on summer vacation and helped when necessary while Diane was at work. Sometimes he would struggle with the buttons on his shirt or spill liquids as he was pouring, but it was all just part of getting stronger as far as Daddy was concerned. I can't remember exactly how long it took for him to fully recover, but I know it was in much less time than the doctors said it would take.

As I mentioned before, I made some poor choices as an early adult and my parents were not happy with me. Although Diane was usually the most vocal about it (and boy was she vocal), I knew Daddy's sentiment was the same. One time when I really messed up and Diane said she washed her hands of me, the following journal entry says it all about my relationship with my father.

Journal Entry 3/26/95- Friday morning Daddy picked me up when I got off from work at 5 am and took me to breakfast. He wanted to talk about getting focused and setting some goals for myself. It made me feel good to know that he is not as an angry as Di. I'm sure he was disappointed, but he said that he doesn't think I'm a lost cause.

THE DETERMINED SHARK

I have one sister, Ruishon. We call her Cherry because she would always turn really red when she cried as a baby. She is two years younger than me, but she acts like she's about 10 years older. While I have always been more playful and happy-go-lucky, my sister is more dramatic and somewhat pensive by comparison, yet quite witty. Though we are pretty different, we have always gotten along very well. We shared a bedroom for the first 10 years of my life, so **I learned a lot about compromise and respecting someone else's space**.

Because I'm older, I've always tried to look out for Cherry. Considering we're fairly close in age, she always returns the favor. With our birth order (and me being a Leo), I've always naturally been in charge in our relationship. As we got older, the few conflicts we've had were mainly because she didn't agree with me (but the Libra in her wasn't sure how to tell me). We still have our share of growing pains, but we are always able to overcome them. Once she came into her own, I backed off and realized that I don't have to be her protector.

Learning to let her flourish and do her own thing came in handy with my employees when I became a manager. Since we are so different and get along so well, I know that is why I easily accept and work with all types of personalities.

My relationship with Cherry has helped me learn to focus on what I have in common with others instead of the differences. Our interests are usually on different parts of the same spectrum with some overlap. For instance, we are both adventurous, except about different things. I'll take physical risks like hang-gliding, roller coasters or jet-skiing. She'll take career risks, like changing companies every few years. I have never met another person who can quit a job one day and easily find a better job the next day as many times as she has.

One of the things I admire most about Cherry is her determination when she really wants something. **She constantly sets goals for herself, does everything it takes to achieve them, then moves on to something else.** If she wants something and doesn't get it right away, then she'll just keep trying until she does. I'll never forget one of the many times we went to a New Edition concert. Upon arrival, we realized the tickets I purchased were an obstructed view of the stage. As the opening acts performed, I became increasingly upset and began brooding because it was clear that we wouldn't be able to fully see New Edition when they performed. The usher wouldn't let us move to the empty section next to us, so I continued to pout. Not Cherry! She talked to that guy for about 10 minutes. I don't know what she said to him, but I know we were able to change seats and enjoy the concert. I'm still not as insistent as she is in that aspect, but it has continued to rub off on me over the years.

THE SUBTLE SHARK IS DETERMINED BUT WILLING TO COMPROMISE

Subtle Shark Exploration

In your career or your business, when is it best to compromise?

When have you felt like giving up, even when it is something you really need?

★ ★ ★ ★ ★ ★ ★ ★ ★ ★ ★

THE NURTURING SHARKS

Growing up, the only adults I spent more time with than my parents were my grandmothers. We call Diane's mother, Grandma and Daddy's mother, Bigma. When we were too young to stay at home alone, we'd hang at Grandma's house until Diane and Daddy got off work. When my parents travelled for my father's job we'd split our time between Grandma's and Bigma's house, aside from regular visits.

Grandma's house was fun because we had a lot more freedom than at home. We could walk around barefoot, get second helpings of dinner and play down the street. The only not-so-fun thing was that we'd have to wash dishes, clean the dining room and take out the garbage before we could go out to play. I guess that's where Diane got it from. It was at Grandma's house where **I learned the valuable lessons of teamwork and prioritizing.** When we were dragging our feet, she would always say, "If we all work together we can finish sooner!" or "If you get your work done quickly and correctly, then you have the rest of the day to play!"

Being at Bigma's house was fun too. Unlike at home and Grandma's house, we didn't have to do any chores. She didn't want us to wash dishes because we may cut ourselves if we broke a glass and she didn't want us to help in the kitchen because we might burn ourselves on the stove. Her overly cautious nature was somewhat annoying when we could only play in the grass and not the sidewalk. We were safe nonetheless!

And though, we ultimately had more freedom at their homes, **Grandma and Bigma instilled a sense of discipline and structure –** because of course, that's where my parents got it from. We dare not give them a hard time, because not only would they make us go "get a switch," but we'd "get it" again once our parents found out.

What I learned from both grandmothers was the spirit of generosity.

Everyone always felt welcomed in their homes and no one ever left hungry. The epitome of southern hospitality, they would give you anything you asked for. I don't claim to be anywhere near as generous as my grandmothers, but **I learned from them to give without an expectation of reciprocation.**

THE SUBTLE SHARK BELIEVES IN SHARED CONTRIBUTION

★ ★ ★ ★ ★ ★ ★ ★ ★ ★ ★

Subtle Shark Exploration

In your career or your business are you only focused on your needs?

What is your definition of teamwork & how do you contribute?

THE HARDWORKING SHARKS

Both Granddaddy (Diane's father) and Pa-Pa (Daddy's father) worked a lot, until I was almost an adult. And even once they got home from their jobs, they were still men of few words. Nonetheless, I felt their love and influence. **From them I learned the importance of hard work and financial responsibility.** They both took care of their families and neither wife had to work if they did not want to. There was no calling off sick or going on disability though they both had very physical jobs. Once when Diane was on the bubble at work, Gramps told her, "Never let anyone force you out of a job. Leave on your own terms." Granddaddy was a World War II veteran and repaired trucks at Fruehauf until he retired. But even before he retired, he opened a neighborhood store called The Pastry Shop that was in business for 33 years.   Pa-Pa was a Korean War veteran and worked at Inland Steel mill until he retired.

They passed down their work ethic to my parents and I have continued the tradition.

CHAPTER ONE'S

SUBTLE SHARK BITES

Some of the qualities I learned from my family were:

Work Ethic   **Integrity**   **Structure**

Determination   **Dependability**   **Compromise**

CHAPTER TWO
NOURISHMENT

Research has shown that sharks are highly intelligent creatures and are very curious about their environment. Shark pups spend the early weeks of their life learning to catch prey and avoid predators so that they can fend for themselves. And unlike some myths about them, they hunt for food, not sport. As a Subtle Shark, I consider my prey to be education and achievement, not other people. I have always liked to learn new things and expound on my current level of knowledge. It is one way I know for sure that I will always be able to fend for myself and stay at the top of my own personal food chain of success.

As far as I'm concerned, knowledge comes in many forms, not just formal education. Yet, the experiences I had while in school helped nourish my appetite for continuous learning.

SUBTLE SHARK BREAKFAST

My elementary school career started out a little differently than most. Because of religious reasons, my parents delayed my vaccination shots for about a year. As a result, I was unable to enroll in school. In the meantime, my cousin Tracey, who is only about four months older than me, was already attending kindergarten and had gone to pre-school. She would teach me everything she was learning. Plus, my parents had already taught me the alphabet. I finally got my shots by age six. I was old enough to be in first grade, but the school insisted that I complete kindergarten first. My parents didn't agree with the decision, but wanted to at least get my foot in the door, so they initially conceded. That only lasted for about a week. My mother, being the persistent person she is, badgered the principal, until they agreed to at least give me a chance to see how I'd do in the first grade. I had a full week to prove that I wasn't educationally and socially behind the rest of the six-year-olds in the class. Like a good mother, Diane gave me a pep talk to let me know how important it was that I did well and that she knew I could do it. From there, it was up to me. I did it and was allowed to stay in first grade! **I stepped up to a challenge to reach the goal.** It gave me such a boost of confidence.

For the next few years, school was a breeze. After first grade, my parents decided they wanted to send me and Cherry to Holy Trinity, a Catholic school. Looking back, one of the things I loved most about the school was that students who read at a higher level than their grade were able to go to the next grade's classroom for Reading and Phonics. So as a second grader, I went to the third grade classroom to take reading.

That was a sense of pride and achievement for me at such a young age.

Additionally, now I got to know my teacher for the next year in advance and interact with older students. For math, we were divided into three groups based on comprehension level. Group 1 consisted of students with the highest understanding. The teacher spent more time with Groups 2 and 3. From 2nd to 4th grade, I was in Group 1. When we began fractions toward the end of 4th grade, I struggled because it didn't build on my previous learning.

Fifth grade was my least favorite year of elementary school. Our teacher was new, so I had to start from scratch with proving myself. I hadn't had to do this since I transferred to Holy Trinity. **In a sense, I guess I felt like my reputation preceded me.** Now this brand new teacher didn't know anything about Ayesha and her capabilities. When she did the math testing to determine which group everyone would be in for the year, I ended up in Group 2 for the first time ever. Doggone fractions! I never verbalized it, but I was emotionally devastated and disappointed in myself. I got A's & B's in math the entire year, whereas if I'd been in Group 1 it would have likely been C's. But at the time I would have preferred the latter if given a choice.

THE SUBTLE SHARK BUILDS A SOLID REPUTATION

Subtle Shark Exploration

What have you done to build a name for yourself in your career or your business?

Do others know who you are and what they can expect from you?

After a disappointing fifth grade year, my universe got back to normal for 6th through 8th grade. The rest of my elementary career, I was always in Group 1 Math. In the last half of my eighth grade year, our school principal started teaching Algebra to Group 1, to get us prepared for high school. I still struggled with fractions because I had never really understood them in 4th grade. My teacher noticed. Instead of relegating me to Group 2, she had another student re-teach me fractions. I don't even think it took him an hour to explain them before I finally got it. It bears mentioning that he was one of the smartest guys in our class and I'd had a crush on him since second grade. And although I was boy-crazy as most 13-year-old girls are, I didn't drag out the tutoring to spend more one-on-one time with him. Why, you ask? Because it was more important for me to be considered smart by my teacher and probably even him. Besides, I didn't want to risk being moved from Group 1 to Group 2. Overall, I maintained my ranking in the top ten of our class. So I was content.

SUBTLE SHARK LUNCH

I went from Holy Trinity Elementary School to Andrean, a Catholic high school, where students are required to take an entrance exam for admittance. I was never nervous about getting in because I had excelled in grade school. But I knew the educational bar had been raised when I found out that they had an "A" honor roll that was separate from the "B" honor roll. I had never come close to straight A's at Holy Trinity. My report card was always an equal balance of A's and B's, with the occasional C.

It was exciting to finally be in high school. I fully embraced the experience, but was challenged academically. My freshman year built on what I'd learned in 8th grade. I earned less A's and B's and more C's than I had been used to, but my parents were more lenient since it was my first year. I struggled quite a bit during sophomore year, and my parents' patience had worn thin. I pretty much stayed on punishment the entire time because each report card got worse. I really didn't apply myself. I was used to doing well in just about every subject without studying, but that was no longer working. **I was too stubborn to change my habits and too proud to ask for help.** It took me a while to realize that as with fractions in the 4th grade, I struggled when new classes did not build on previous subject-matter. My first semester ended with a B, five C's and my very first ever D in geometry. My grades improved slightly in the second semester when we got a new geometry teacher.

THE SUBTLE SHARK ASKS FOR HELP AND ADAPTS TO CHANGE

★ ★ ★ ★ ★ ★ ★ ★ ★ ★ ★ ★

Subtle Shark Exploration

What big changes are you experiencing in your career or your business?

Are you being honest with yourself about whether or not you need help?

★ ★ ★ ★ ★ ★ ★ ★ ★ ★ ★ ★

By my junior year, **I had learned my lesson and was determined** that I wasn't going to spend another school year on punishment because of my grades. I started out strong with all A's & B's, except for a C in Journalism (I swear that teacher just didn't like me!), making the "B" Honor Roll in the first quarter. Then I fell in love and spent more time on the phone than studying. I ended up with C's in three of seven classes at the end of the first semester. Again I was on punishment. I bounced back quickly and made the B honor roll again in the 3rd quarter.

I had struggled all year in Algebra II, even though I was actually studying. **Finally I asked a good friend to tutor me** during our downtime in gym class. By the end of the year I again had A's and B's with only one C, which was in Algebra II. **I should have asked for help sooner** because I got a B on the exam thanks to my tutor, but it wasn't enough to save my cumulative grade.

My senior year of high school was bittersweet. Academically I was <u>finally</u> back to my former glory, but emotionally it was rough because I was having romantic problems. I spent a lot of time that year upset over a silly boy, but my grades had never been better. I made the B honor roll every quarter, with all A's and B's at the end of the first semester. I applied to Purdue University and was wait-listed due to my horrible math grades from the first two and a half years of high school. Thankfully, I aced Trigonometry, and was finally admitted in February of my senior year.

SUBTLE SHARK DINNER

After graduating high school in the top half of my class, I went to Purdue University, West Lafayette that fall. Living on a college campus was liberating and lots of fun. I majored in Management and ended up with four A's and two C's in the first semester. I was even invited to join a freshman honor society. I struggled during the second semester in my first college level accounting class, Management 200. I hadn't met anyone who didn't have to take it at least twice. **As a result, I studied in that class; something I finally realized was necessary when the subject didn't come easily to me.** I even took the practice tests offered in an effort to do well. Unfortunately, chemistry was no joke either. I ended up getting F's in both, which was the first time I flunked a class.

So I retook Management 200 and ended up getting a C! Now the problem was that chemistry was replaced with physics and I was taking my first real computer class. Keep in mind that this was back in 1990, when barely any households had a PC. So I'm sorry to say I flunked two more classes. At that point my parents decided they would no longer pay for my college education. It was a replay of my sophomore year in high school and they weren't going to waste their money.

Although, I had actually put in effort this time, I couldn't blame them for doubting it, based on my track record.

Diane even talked to me about possibly changing my major. But I really wanted to conquer this challenge and wouldn't consider it. The second semester of sophomore year was a little better, since I only flunked one class.

That summer at home wasn't pretty. My parents were more than a little perturbed with me. I figured they no longer had a say in what I did, considering they weren't paying my tuition. Although I was still living under their roof, rent free. (Teenagers!) My sister had just graduated from high school and would attend Purdue as well. Cherry, being the social butterfly she is, met and introduced me to more people in the month before school started than I had met the previous two years there. Parties became a priority.   I had registered for school, but didn't even have enough credits to qualify as a junior since I had flunked so many classes and was on academic probation. By then, I had mentally checked out on my scholastic career. After a couple of months, I stopped going to my classes and eventually flunked out of college. I had let myself down and felt like my parents had given up on me. My sister went back home after her first semester, but I had gotten used to my independence and decided to stay in West Lafayette. Diane and Daddy went along with it for a few months. But I didn't have a Plan B or a job, so they made me come back home. I felt like such a failure!

THE SUBTLE SHARK LEARNS FROM MISTAKES AND TRIES AGAIN

★ ★ ★ ★ ★ ★ ★ ★ ★ ★ ★ ★

Subtle Shark Exploration

What professional failures are you facing?

What is your plan to learn from them and start over?

SUBTLE SHARK DESSERT

It took over seven years to decide to pursue a college degree again. I started working full time shortly after coming home from West

Lafayette, so school was the furthest thing from my mind. Seemingly, out of the blue, early in 1999 I started getting that itch. We had begun a family investment group several years prior and were doing pretty well with it. This made me start to think about my future. As we discussed what we would do with our budding wealth, I shared one of my dreams, which is to build a day care/community/after school facility. Initially part of my plan was to get a degree in Early Childhood Education. I was accepted into Purdue University-Calumet, which was close to home, but far from work. While I contemplated the scheduling and commuting conflicts, I enrolled in the online program at the University of Phoenix instead.

I was proud of myself for getting back on the horse.

At that time my job experiences overlapped with much of the subject matter. So I was able to apply some of the theories I learned to either support or refute them based on reality. **It took a lot of self-discipline to take online classes, but I was focused this time**, even with the full-time job. It was actually taking longer than the two years I thought I needed to get my degree. So when I hit that 24th month, I was burned out and took a 30-day break. Unfortunately, that month turned into almost two years. Once I re-enrolled, I was determined not to take anymore "breaks," earning my degree in 2005. I was disappointed in myself for flunking out of Purdue. But I believe everything happens for a reason. Because I was able to immediately apply what I was learning in school to my job, my degree means so much to me now.

CHAPTER TWO'S

SUBTLE SHARK BITES

My formal education taught me the following:

Everything will not come easily

It is okay to ask for help

Do not get discouraged by failure

CHAPTER THREE
CATCH AND RELEASE

When sharks are searching for food they utilize three different methods. The "hit and run" is where one bite is enough for the shark, usually because it does not taste like their normal food source. The "bump and bite" is exactly how it sounds. Sharks first bump the victim, then continually returns for more bites. Lastly is the "sneak attack," where the shark appears with no warning and takes bite after bite. I liken these three processes to how I finally settled on my occupation. A few of my jobs were like the "hit and run." I took them because I needed the money, but only remained for a short time. There were a couple of "bump and bite" employments when I was committed for longer instances, but had no desire to make them extended situations. By the time I had graduated from high school, I knew I wanted to go into management, but had no idea what it really entailed, or how I would get there. My "sneak" attack was when my last part-time job blossomed into a career; something I could see myself doing for the rest of my working life.

BAIT

My first taxpaying job was while I was attending Purdue. Although my parents were paying my tuition at the time, they wanted me to gain experience and earn money for any extra activities. I still remember my very first day. I was assigned to the beverage room and my trainer was a sophomore and Waiter Captain, *Woody. He didn't take things very seriously, but always did a good job. He explained to me that captains were responsible for assigning tasks, helping out in busy areas and inspecting to make sure all duties were complete before dismissing waiters at the end of the shift. **Though I had just started, I set it as a future goal to become a Waiter Captain before I graduated. I made sure I learned all of the different areas and got pretty good at the job.**

During my first year as a waiter, another student, *Velma, was promoted to Captain and let the power go to her head. She was condescending, didn't help out and was full of herself. None of us liked working with her, and a few of us got together and added the acronym "W.A.V." to our name tags. It stood for "Waiters Against *Velma." One of the adult supervisors got wind of it after a few weeks and made us remove it. But I had already decided that I would not be like *Velma when I got promoted. Other Captains who were a lot more like *Woody, were fun to work with, while still making sure the job got done.

When I achieved my goal the following year of becoming a Captain, I decided to model my leadership style after them.

My promotion wasn't about bossing people around. It was about doing less physical work and being in a position to make decisions that would help the shift run smoothly. It was my first taste of being "in charge" and I enjoyed it.

HIT AND RUN

The summer after my freshman year, my parents made me work while I was home. My godmother was the location manager of a Wendy's and gave jobs to me, Cherry and Tracey. By then I had a year of work experience, but it still didn't prepare me for fast food. Although it was still food service, working at Wendy's was a world of difference from the cafeteria. Now I was dealing with paying customers, who got to choose how they wanted their food prepared, who didn't clean up after themselves and didn't necessarily have to be nice to you – all while working in a hot, greasy kitchen. It was at Wendy's where **I learned about customer service, quickly resolving issues (like incorrect orders), handling large sums of money and constantly cleaning up after others.** Unlike the dorm cafeteria, the people I served at Wendy's had a choice of where they were going to eat that day. I made sure their experience was a pleasant one. It was a lot of work for $3.80 per hour, which was minimum wage in 1990. Over the next couple of years, I worked at Burger King, Arby's and a local pizza shop, all for less than $5.00 per hour. It was some of the hardest, most thankless work I have ever done in my entire career. But, I did learn how to hustle because the "fast" in fast food was not a misnomer. People expected to be served quickly and accurately. Job specialization in fast food was nonexistent. **It was important to learn every role so that you could fill in whenever necessary. It was the epitome of multi-tasking.**

THE SUBTLE SHARK GAINS EXPERIENCE THEN MOVES FORWARD

Subtle Shark Exploration

Your career or business may not yet be where you'd like, but what experience are you gaining that will help you get there?

What is your plan for getting to the next level?

★ ★ ★ ★ ★ ★ ★ ★ ★ ★ ★

SNEAK ATTACK

Although I had only officially been in the workforce for three years, I felt like a veteran when I was finally able to graduate from food service to retail in 1992 as I went to work for Best Buy. Daddy had been in the job hunt for a couple of months when he came across an ad in the paper that an electronics retailer was hiring in our area. At the time, Best Buy was just entering the Chicagoland market and only had about 30 stores nationally.

The hiring process was a little cumbersome because we actually had to take a skill assessment, in addition to filling out the application. Daddy applied in computers and I applied to be a cashier. While the actual store was under construction, we trained in a nearby hotel. Once the store was ready to be stocked, we started merchandising. With the Grand Opening approaching, overtime was being offered to anyone willing.

Daddy told me that whenever your job offers extra hours never turn it down because it shows initiative and you don't know when things will get lean. I was convinced because I wanted to make enough to be able to quit Wendy's.

The store opened in September of 1992 to a lot of fanfare and stayed extremely busy all the time. The store's management team consisted of *Campbell (General Manager), *Norm (Operations), *Vanessa (Sales) and *James (Inventory). **Campbell was very engaging, pleasant and knowledgeable**; it didn't hurt that he was easy on the eyes. Though he was always very busy, he often chatted with the employees. I'll never forget one instance when my father was limping as he walked passed (a reflection of Daddy's hip problems) and *Campbell stopped him with a very concerned look on his face. *Campbell said, "Leland, I see you have a little hitch in your giddy up!" They talked for a few minutes as Daddy assured him that he'd be okay. That sticks out in my mind because for one, I had never before heard the phrase "hitch in your giddy up" and secondly *Campbell had the entire store to worry about, but stopped what he was doing and seemed genuinely concerned. *Norm, as the Operations Manager, hired me, and was unofficially my first professional mentor. He was a lot more intense than *Campbell, but still liked to have fun as long as the work was being done. *Vanessa's demeanor was similar to *Norm, but she was even more no nonsense than he. *James was really laid back, but still took care of his business. I always enjoyed working on his shifts because nothing ever rattled him. He rarely ever got agitated. He was like a fun uncle. Customer service had two supervisors, *Jane and *Tomasina. *Jane also balanced taking care of business with having fun. *Tomasina was the exact opposite. She panicked about everything and always appeared stressed out.

THE SUBTLE SHARK LEARNS FROM GOOD AND BAD LEADERS

Subtle Shark Exploration

What positive traits are you learning from other professionals that will help your career or business?

What have you learned NOT to do?

BUMP AND BITE

With all the overtime during the first few months at Best Buy, I was able to quit Wendy's. Less than a year later, the OT dried up. With my college debt and household expenses mounting, I sought another part-time job. Cherry was employed by a gas station chain, Welsh and told me they were hiring at another location. I started working there as a cashier. Thankfully the pace was much slower than what I was used to at Best Buy and fast food. It was a good second job to have.

CHAPTER THREE'S

SUBTLE SHARK BITES

Some of the skills I learned from my first jobs were:

Customer Service

Basic Leadership

Employee Follow Up

28

CHAPTER FOUR
SHARK ATTACK

It may surprise some that sharks are not territorial creatures. They do not defend large sections of the ocean. However, they will defend the area around them and attack those who invade their space. When sharks are hunting for food, they stalk their prey (far enough away to be hidden, but close enough to seize opportunity). I took this same approach when mapping out my career path. Once I started working for Best Buy and saw the chance for advancement, I was quietly on the hunt for the next attack. It wasn't about getting to the highest ranking job in the store (the ocean), but what was next in line for me (my space). Excelling at my job was always the first mission, while watching and learning from whoever was in the future position that I sought (stalking prey). Hopefully, they were good enough at their job that they would soon be promoted, enabling me to strike when the opening occurred.

IN THE HUNT

I was a pretty good cashier (CSR 1), thanks to my fast food days. It just wasn't challenging enough. My eyes were set on working at the service desk as a Customer Service Representative 2 (CSR2) as soon as possible. Within the first week or so, I had the opportunity to prove myself because the seniors and supervisors would let CSR1s fill in when CSR2s took breaks. **I volunteered to fill in every chance I got and learned as much as I could while I was there.** I gave myself the same pep talk Diane gave me when I had the chance to skip kindergarten. Thankfully, the store was so busy all the time that they started hiring and promoting people almost immediately. Within 30 days, I earned a CSR2 position. It was a true test of my abilities because I was responsible for answering phones, ringing returns/exchanges, testing product, and processing financing applications among many other things. I enjoyed the challenge.

Shortly after becoming a CSR2, I set my sights on the Customer Service Senior position. They were responsible for supplying change for the registers, assigning and covering breaks/lunches, doing month end reports and performing opening/closing duties when the supervisors weren't scheduled. It was similar to my job as a Waiter Captain in college, so I knew I could handle it. **I wanted to place myself as a top contender for when the job opened.** I always finished my transactions quickly to be available to volunteer for additional things. I paid attention to the tasks the "sups" and seniors completed when performing opening and closing duties. Often, I'd asked to do my own or to help with another cashier's paperwork for practice. When the senior position opened in November, guess who applied for and got the job as a result? Yep! This shark! Two promotions in two months is impressive, if I must say so myself. Though I had prepared for the position, it didn't come without its hurdles. It was a lot more responsibility, which took some getting used to. *Jane did a good job of coaching me and holding me accountable when necessary. **She required me to set goals for myself and write them down so we could work on them together.** A couple of months later, *Norm and *Campbell were transferred to different stores within several weeks of each other. Now I felt like I was going to have to start over with proving myself to new managers. It was like fifth grade again. Additionally, *Tomasina was annoying as a micromanager. But I worked through it.

The next goal: Become a supervisor. **Since I had mastered all of the customer service jobs, I began helping the in-store technician.** Although his job title suggested otherwise, he wasn't allowed to fix anything. He tested returned and exchanged products to determine if it could go back to the sales floor or be shipped out for repair. He also programmed and activated cell phones after they were purchased. This was back in the day when they were the sizes of bricks and cost three times as much as they do now.

Working with the tech served two purposes, the first of which was increasing my skill level.

Secondly, he had no back up for his job. Work was left for him to do on his next scheduled shift. It never sat well with me for customers to wait an extra day to get their phones. He would program several in advance for us to have in his absence, but it was never enough. So I learned how to program them myself. I never wanted to become an in-store technician but I knew it would be a feather in my cap to have first-hand knowledge of that job when a supervisor position opened up.

THE SUBTLE SHARK PREPARES FOR THE NEXT OPPORTUNITY

Subtle Shark Exploration

What is the next step in your career or business?

How will you know when it is time to actively pursue it?

LEARNING THE OCEAN CURRENTS

Six months after the store opened, *Jane got accepted into the management training program (MIT). I just knew that becoming a supervisor was right around the corner for me. Unfortunately, things took a different turn. Two jobs opened in the customer service department when *Jane left, one for supervisor and one for senior. After waiting a week to be interviewed, I was told by the new Operations Manager, *Beau, that his decision was to add two seniors instead of one and not fill the second supervisor position. Get this... he said it was because *Tomasina felt like she would have a better opportunity to get promoted in the near future if she was the sole supervisor. I was livid! She never hid the fact that she was unhappy when she wasn't accepted into the management program and *Jane was. My other thoughts were: 1)*Tomasina didn't stand a chance of getting promoted, so now she was in the way of my goals and 2) Instead of only being in competition with one other senior when the supervisor position finally opened, I'd be in the running with the two new ones. I considered quitting at that time. To make matters worse, *Tomasina was training everyone but me on making schedules and other supervisor duties.

I think this was my first experience with what I consider to be "office politics" and it wasn't a good feeling.

In the meantime, we found out that *Vanessa would be our co-Operations Manager with *Beau. I had worked a few shifts with her as the manager on duty and we got along pretty well. As it turns out, she was big on employee development. **She had us write out our goals, and let her know what we wanted to learn to further improve our skills.**

My relationship with *Tomasina rapidly deteriorated after she gave me a hard time about getting the second job and the sole supervisor situation. I had completely lost the little bit of respect I had left for her. As a result, I wasn't the most pleasant person in our interactions. I never acted disrespectfully, but it probably came close a few times. One of those times, she noticed and pulled me aside. I let her know that it upset me when she called me out for situations I had no control over. Of course, she apologized and made up excuses, but the damage was done. A few weeks after starting my part-time job is when I decided that I was going to "secretly" take over the department from *Tomasina.

Looking back on it, that mindset was immature, but I was so fed up with her lack of leadership.

She played favorites, she was never around when we needed her, she didn't follow up on anything, and she was never forthcoming with information. I felt like I knew what needed to be done in the department, and it was time to start working around her to get things done the right way. I began my reconstruction of customer service with things that were long overdue to be handled and would help the department run more efficiently. I did it for my own peace of mind. **I finally realized that "acting out" wasn't getting me anywhere or improving and expanding my knowledge.** Besides, this would be a time to show my potential.

Meanwhile, the store's new general manager, *Martin facilitated management training sessions with senior-level and above. I participated in this great opportunity to increase my skills and learn more about how the other departments of the store functioned.

*Journal Entry July 11, 1993- *Avery gave me helpful hints on how to move up and be successful (make a list of the things I want to accomplish). He has some good philosophies and a good outlook. I really admire him. I hope he's in our store long enough for me to learn everything from him that I can.*

The person mentioned above was only around for a couple of months before being promoted to store manager, but made a lasting impression on just about everyone in the location. He was the first manager I had ever encountered who knew what was going on in all departments and pitched in wherever he saw a need. **I decided I would take advantage and learn all that I could when opportunities to help out in other departments came up.** As a result, I assisted on the sales floor and in the warehouse when it wasn't busy in customer service.

*Journal Entry July 14, 1993- I know I am in competition with *Erica for the supervisor position. And although we are basically running the department together ourselves, she has the upper-hand. If she got promoted, it would be that much longer for me to have to wait. I need to at least give her a run for her money and right now I don't feel like I'm doing that. I've decided that I want to be exactly like *Avery, on a smaller scale for now. I want to know something about everything, make an impact, be efficient and get the job done. I feel like I've come a long way over the last couple of months, but I still have a ways to go. To get my goals accomplished I need to list them out, list how I can get them done, give myself a time limit and do it.*

In August of 1993, *Tomasina had to take six weeks of sick leave. The good part was obvious. The bad part was *Erica was named acting supervisor and not me.

In the midst of the past five months, I had lost my unofficial position of being the number one senior in the department.

Although *Erica was really good at the job, I think I let myself get too distracted with my personal life, my part-time job and my attitude with *Tomasina. As a result of focusing on the negative, my own performance started to slip.

THE SUBTLE SHARK DOES NOT GET DISTRACTED BY NEGATIVITY

Subtle Shark Exploration

What outside influences are you allowing to distract you from your goals?

What do you need to do to regain focus?

*Journal Entry August 5, 1993- I feel as though I have a lot to prove to *Vanessa because she is my manager. I do think that I have been doing a very good job, but there is definitely room for improvement. I actually think my major problem is the little things. I need to practice follow up and finish out. I have been practicing, so now it's just a matter of perfecting it. Another key is making the most of the time I am given. I have improved at that also. I know that I have to bust my butt to get recognition. It's not that *Erica worked so much harder than me, she just comes across as flawless.*

It made me feel less stressed when soon after the above journal entry, *Erica got promoted to a supervisor position in a new store.

*Journal Entry 8/13/93- Today we found out that *Vanessa is transferring & we're getting an Ops Manager from Indianapolis. I am highly upset: #1 I busted my butt proving myself to *Vanessa, #2 *Tomasina gets to start with a clean slate and #3 we have to start over from scratch.*

*Vanessa's replacement was a nice enough guy, but didn't really make an impact on my development. A few months later *Martin was demoted and transferred to another location because of some theft issues that were going on in the store. It was sad to see him go under those circumstances, but over the past year, *Norm had been promoted to general manager at a different location. He ended up being transferred back to our store to replace *Martin. I was really excited to work with him again. Systematically and quickly, he broke up what turned out to be a theft ring that had been plaguing the store.

Soon after, like clockwork, the latest operations manager transferred. So I was on my fifth one in a little over a year. But the new guy, *Jesse, ended up being one of my favorite managers. I used to call him "Okie Skokie" because he was from a small town in Minnesota and was naïve about pop culture. He was very engaged with the department. He liked to joke around, but knew when it was time to get down to business. If any issues arose, he addressed them immediately. **By then *Tomasina's incompetence no longer consumed me. I was focused again and had another good manager to learn from.** Although it was fun working with *Jesse, I was getting antsy about becoming a supervisor. I had been a senior for over 1 ½ years and everyone in other departments was getting promoted around me. So I applied for a customer service supervisor position at store that was about an hour away.

*Journal Entry 4/15/94- There's a job opening for Ops Sup at Joliet. I'm scared to apply because I may get it. This distance alone is going to put a strain on our transportation situation. *Norm and *Jesse don't want me to go and understandably so. I am the glue to this operations department. Hopefully *Thomasina's days are numbered.*

*Journal Entry 4/28/94- I had my interview with *Rob yesterday and I think it went rather well. He seemed impressed with a lot of my answers. He kept reiterating how highly *Jesse & *Norm spoke of me. I am one of 3 candidates, so my chances are good. I'll find out either way, today or tomorrow at the latest. *Tomasina has ticked *Jesse off because she threw away a customer's unit.*

*Journal Entry 5/1/94- Since I last wrote, *Tomasina got suspended. It's looking like she'll get demoted, which means I'll be promoted. The deal will probably go down Wednesday. I still haven't heard anything from *Rob about Joliet. I'm going send him an email tomorrow.*

Journal Entry 5/13/94- I was officially named Ops Sup on Wednesday. I pray that I do the best job I can possibly do and make myself proud.

CHAPTER FOUR'S

SUBTLE SHARK BITES

To be the top contender for any position:

Learn all you can about other jobs

Maintain superior performance in your current job

Stay focused on what you can control

Study your leaders and look for good traits that you can emulate

CHAPTER 5
EBB AND FLOW

Existing at the top of their food chain means that sharks are responsible for creating an ecological balance in their environment. That's how I felt when I finally earned the operations supervisor position. As much as I thought I had been doing *Tomasina's job before, it was nothing like having the full weight of a department on my shoulders. Working for her really enhanced my craving for fairness and consistency (ecological balance); receiving it and ensuring it for whoever I worked with. I already knew that **managing others wasn't about barking orders, but getting everyone to work together toward a common goal**. My leadership skills blossomed because I had absorbed great examples of it from positive role models, like oxygenated water through shark gills. But over the next year and half my journey saw some highs and lows that really tested my confidence, balance and skills.

HIGH TIDES

Journal Entry 6/2/94- With my promotion comes another level of maturity that I need to apply to all areas of my life. At work 85% of my department seems to be testing me. I'm at a boiling point now, ready to explode. With all the call-offs, I haven't had enough time to get the department as organized as I'd planned. So my 1st solution is to get some more people in. Hopefully by the end of June, everything will be in place like I want it. There are so many issues I need to stay on top of.

My promotion to Operations Supervisor taught me a valuable lesson.

I learned that you never truly know what a position entails until you are doing it 100% of the time.

As a senior, I was only exposed to bits and pieces during my shift. The supervisor is responsible for everything that goes on in the department, even when they're not present.

*Journal Entry 8/9/94- Things are going pretty decently at work. We're still short-handed, but managing pretty well. Now that *Erica is back as a senior, I can set some ground rules for the seniors to run the department. In the meantime, I'll be able to set some more programs in place and learn some more management stuff. They were taking applications for MIT this past week, but both *Norm and I felt that I wasn't ready. I did apply for CO-OP trainer for D-27. I'm not sure how soon I'll be hearing about it though. I really enjoy my job.   Right now I'm going to concentrate on furthering my career w/BB. Over the next 6 months things should be moving pretty fast for me & I want to be more than prepared. I plan to be ready for and accepted to MIT by early spring. MY GOALS:*
<u>For my department</u>-Develop and implement game plan on how I want my department to run; Keep a watchful eye to maintain order; Effective discipline; No procrastination; Make sure that what needs to get done is done!!!
<u>As key senior</u>-Keep learning and implementing; Do one thing at a time; Keep and follow a to do list; Minimize play time; No procrastination

I usually scheduled myself a 12pm to 8pm shift at Best Buy, and worked 9pm to 5am at Welsh 2-3 times per week. Working a mid-shift allowed me to interact with all of my team members at some point during the day. I had to make sure processes were in place, everyone was trained properly and handle constant employee turnover. Additionally, *Norm made me a "Key Senior" a few months into the position. Officially, I was still a supervisor, but I was given managers' computer access and the responsibility of opening and closing the store from time to time. I didn't get any adjustment in pay, **but I appreciated the opportunity to get a feel for management without the full-on pressure of the job.** I was in no rush for another promotion anytime soon. Over the past couple of years, I had built pretty good working relationships with most of the employees in the store. And as I mentioned before, **I helped out in other departments to increase my knowledge, with the added perk of having earned their respect.** So as Key Senior, I had no friction with the other supervisors who were basically my peers and subordinates at the same time.

*Journal Entry 4/6/95- I found out last Friday that this upcoming Monday I would be in MIT. I had absolutely no choice in the matter. It all started that Wednesday when *Norm sprung on me that *Luca was coming here as Ops Sup. This (supposedly) left *Norm with a bunch of choices with what to do with me. He informed me that whatever he decided, I'd have no choice in the matter. When he told me my fate Friday, he tried to make it sound like he did it for me. I let him know that I didn't ask for it. I feel bad leaving my department high & dry. For a person who didn't have to apply or interview to get into MIT, I should feel lucky, but I don't.*

It's important to note that sometime between the last entry and the end of that same month,*Norm was transferred to another store and replaced by *Nelson.

MIT went pretty well. Aside from being exhausted on the days I worked my second job, I enjoyed the experience. I realized I knew a lot already, and learned even more about the retail business. In hindsight, not much was taught about leadership, but I had implemented what I was learning from my managers.

*Journal Entry 5/16/95- Work is a little less hectic now that I'm done with MIT. *Nelson hired *Maggie as our Ops Manager, which is fine with me. He said that we will be building our mega store this year. So I'm excited about the prospect of OT. *Nelson seems to be okay so far, we'll see. Me and *Maggie should be able to get along fine if she leaves me alone and lets me do my job. Hopefully I can stick to my plans and not become a manager until next year.*

LOW TIDES

What follows are several journal entries with no commentary in between because they were very detailed and paint the picture of what took place over the next six months.

*Journal Entry 7/24/95- Right now I'm awaiting a decision that could mean a forward career move for me. *Norm called me Wednesday to inform me of an Ops Mgr position opening in his store. He warned that the culture is tough and that if he found a more qualified applicant that's who he'd go with. He came into the store Sunday afternoon. He sat me down to again warn me about the clientele and the employees. He was talking almost like I had the position, but he did keep saying "if". He said his biggest concern would be handling the change of personalities. I told him to do what he feels is right, but he'd never know what I'm capable of unless he gave me a chance. Personally I think I'd be up to the challenge. As long as I know I'm right and* *feel like I have support, I can go up against anyone. Whether I get it or not, I'll be happy. Becoming an Ops Mgr would mean a raise, more authority, the opportunity to become part of a mega store, working w/*Norm and a step toward an even more promising future. Not to mention, I could quit working at Welsh and still be able to afford to live. Yet, if I don't get the position, I won't be disappointed. It'll give me the chance to continue developing my ladies and implement some of the plans I made. I wouldn't feel like I had unfinished business left to take care of. There's a definite degree of safety. Although I wasn't in a rush before to become a manager, things seem to be different now. *Norm is my "retail godfather. Working for him would give me a feeling of comfort. He knows me and my work ethic pretty well. I've already proven myself as a senior & sup & almost as a manager. He's been there to give me the development I need. I really think this move would be right in time for my change of style and new outlook on life. I really want this.*

Journal Entry 7/29/95- Yesterday was my last day as Operations Supervisor. Tuesday at 8am begins my new venture as Operations Manager. I am so excited. My department threw me a going away party Friday in the conference room. I'm really going to miss my ladies. They really worked their butts off for me. I'm just so excited that I have this opportunity. I plan to make the most of it. D&D are so proud, and I'm proud of myself. Now after almost 3 years at Merrillville, I'm going to another store. I'm going to have to get used to almost 100 new people. I'm going to have to earn respect all over again and build a new reputation. These people don't know me or my style and we're all going to have to get used to each other. They're going to have to take me seriously as a manager. I'm just going to have to be careful in my approach. I am really looking forward to this challenge.

*Journal Entry 8/14/95- I've been manager for 15 days now. It seems to me like I handled the adjustment pretty well. I closed by myself Friday and opened by myself Saturday. That in itself wasn't such a feat, but it was complicated with the truck Friday and nine call-offs Saturday. It could have been stressful, but I wouldn't let it. I'm proud of myself. *Norm called at 12:30 pm Saturday and was surprised that I hadn't called him at home. He said everyone else would have called him at least once by then. I figured if the store isn't burning down, there's no need to call him. Anything short of a natural disaster, I can handle myself. The customer issues aren't anything that I'm not used to. I have a good amount of experience in dealing with most problems. Overall, the customer service department is pretty knowledgeable. But they need to work on their efficiency and phone answering skills. Also, the seniors need to "run" the department. In a lot of ways there's not enough unity. I think a department meeting that sets the expectation would help considerably. I haven't jumped in with both feet yet* *when it comes to running the floor. I mean, I walk it and assist customers, but as far as providing direction for the product specialists, I don't feel comfortable yet. I feel I'm still in the process of earning respect. It's going to take some time, but I feel like I'm going in the right direction. With the store problems we're still fixing, inventory on 9/10, the move on 10/27 and Christmas around the corner, I'm going to have my hands full until at least February.*

*Journal Entry 10/2/95- The only thing going on in my life is work right now. It's been nonstop since I got back from vacation on September 7th. Inventory was on Sunday 9/10, so I was at work from 9am to 3:30 am. Then I had to turn around and come back at 9am because I was running the job fair. I worked the job fair 9am-7pm, Monday-Friday. Saturday was my first day off. We extended the job fair, so I worked it again Monday-Wednesday and I had to close Wednesday night. I had Thursday off, for the only day off that week. *Norm wanted me to have the new people hired by October 1st, but we lost 2 days because the fax machine was down. We have a tentative itinerary through grand opening. *Norm said we may be doing 6-7 days per week until then. It's not like I have a life or anything.*

*Journal Entry 10/3/95- Today at work was slightly stressful. I got 10 emails about new hire and customer service problems. Most of them from *Francis about things she could have handled herself. She's just trying to make me look bad. I guess I have remote controls for everyone that I have hired. Then *Norm sends me a nasty email, like I can single handedly get drug tests and criminal background checks back in less than 24 hours.*

THE SUBTLE SHARK REALIZES EVERY OPPORTUNITY IS NOT THE BEST ONE

★ ★ ★ ★ ★ ★ ★ ★ ★ ★ ★

Subtle Shark Exploration

What are you being offered that doesn't fit your plan or skills?

What "good" chances have you realized are not good for you?

*Journal Entry 11/12/95- Work is moving along. I had started to feel like I was drowning. I felt like I was falling further and further behind in my work. Di said it's mostly about time management. If I can just get totally caught up and then develop a concrete daily, weekly and monthly plan, I can feel more efficient. I can't go into the Christmas season already behind. Di made a good point about focusing on the things that come down directly from *Norm, district and corporate. If I complete those tasks then I'll feel like I got more accomplished.*

*Journal Entry 12/12/95- *Janet was demoted today, so *Norm will be happy. That will keep him off my back for a while. *Janet has already begun to bad-mouth the situation. It's nothing unexpected, I've decided I'm not going to let it bother me. I'm not in this to make any friends or win a popularity contest. I need to keep my job and the only way to do it is to keep my GM happy (within reason). I'm going to have to stay on *Phoebe to keep this department together throughout all of this. She may not be too far from losing her position either. We'll see.*

Whew! I didn't have any more journal entries as Operations Manager after this one, mainly because things went so haywire that I didn't have the time to write. Demoting *Janet was what *Norm wanted me to do, but not what I felt was right at the time. And to make a move like that during the holiday season just didn't make sense to me.

She wasn't given enough time to improve. In addition, I didn't have a chance to work with her and no one was trained to replace her.

It was up to me and the supervisor, *Phoebe, to cover *Janet's duties. Unfortunately, *Phoebe wasn't doing too well as far as her job was concerned either.   I should have spoken up and at least shared my concerns with *Norm. To make a bad situation worse, *Phoebe quit without notice a week before Christmas. The biggest slap in the face was that her replacement was determined by *Norm, without any input from me at all – a pretty big blow from an ego standpoint. She came highly recommended from another location, but I couldn't understand why. She had absolutely no leadership skills. She rarely communicated directly with any of the employees and spent most of her time either in the office or smoking in the break room. I would repeatedly have to track her down to get her to handle things in the department.

Here's the timeline of events during my first few months as a manager:

- August 1995-Received promotion; Transferred to new location
- September 1995-Responsible for Job Fair and staffing
  - (20-30 people) for store relocation & expansion
- October 1995- New Hire Orientations; preparing for relocation
  - (we had two staffs at two locations)
- November 1995-Store relocation & expansion
- December 1995-Christmas Season in Retail (enough said)
- January 1996-Post-Holiday recovery

Within the first six months of my promotion, I faced challenges and major business initiatives that most managers may have encountered over the course of five years. Staffing a store expansion was a full-time job in itself, and we worked 6-7 days per week from that point until the Grand Re-Opening.

There was no time for employee development and establishing accountability in the Operations Department.

As I wrote in my journal, *Norm warned me about the change in store culture I would experience with my transfer. He also expressed his concern with me being able to handle it. In retrospect, it's clear that he doubted my abilities and micromanaged me as a result. And since I considered him my "retail godfather" and was appreciative of him giving me the opportunity, **I didn't challenge him when I should have.**
*Norm was transferred to that store to fix it, just as he had done before. I believe his purpose was to weed out the underperformers and he needed a management team to support him in that task.

During that tumultuous period in my career, I learned so much about myself. I didn't know it then, but I am not that type of manager.

My preference is to work with people and help them release their potential. There are employees who are cast in the wrong role and probably will never be able to do well in a particular type of position. In that case, I wouldn't try to force a square peg into a round hole. But I at least want to give them a chance first. **Yet the fact of the matter is, everyone does not have that level of patience and some situations do**

not allow for it. I am not sure what the circumstances were, but the "house" was going to get cleaned out whether I cooperated or not. *Norm's patience was wearing thin with me and it was obvious as he started making decisions for my department. He had been in the store for about four months before bringing me over, so he had already observed who the difficult employees were. Although it had only been six months for me, it was almost a year for him and I wasn't moving fast enough to fix the problems. In actuality, I only had about one month to get to know my employees (August 1995), maybe another month to set expectations (if you combine any downtime in September, October and November when we weren't doing the job fair, inventory and relocation), and maybe another month to hold people accountable to the newly established expectations (if you combine downtime during the holiday season). Some managers may have done a better job fulfilling those expectations with so many extraneous activities going on, but I doubt they would have been newly promoted and newly transferred.

My department was in turmoil. Yet, I still had to open or close the store, help in other departments and run the floor as the manager on duty on my scheduled days, 50-60 hours per week. Then on my "days off," I came in to try to get my department in order. During the entire month of January I took about 3 days off and was absolutely miserable.

I was failing as a manager and close to losing my job. *Norm reached out to *Jane, who was now the General Manager of the local service repair center to see if she had any job openings. I knew very little about repairs, but was not in a position to be picky. I got the customer service job pretty easily. I was disappointed in my demotion, but able to take a step back to re-evaluate my career path, minus all the pressure. Diane was upset and felt like I hadn't fought hard enough to keep my management position. At that point I was exhausted and just couldn't do it anymore. I took a couple of days off and started at the service center at the end of the month.

CHAPTER FIVE'S

SUBTLE SHARK BITES

Some of the challenges I faced were:

Thinking you know a job before you are actually

doing it full time

Knowing when to speak up and respectfully

challenge your boss

Understanding what to expect when going into a completely

new environment

CHAPTER SIX
OPEN WATER

Sharks can rapidly adapt to new environments when searching for food, but most cannot survive in fresh water. During my miniscule time as manager, I quickly learned it's possible to collapse under a massive load when in an inhospitable environment. Because sharks evolved in salt water, to drop them in fresh water can be deadly.

I was still evolving and wasn't quite ready for a management position, especially under those circumstances (fresh water).

After getting back to the ocean, it was time for me to start over and attempt to survive as I ventured into somewhat uncharted territory. I was still in operations where I had begun. I may have been wounded, but my rehabilitation would be swift.

SUBMERGED

Needless to say, I was completely disillusioned by my short stint as manager and felt like a total failure. But a part of me was relieved to be away from the pressure of having to "fix" a department under someone else's terms.

Transferring from the crazy, chaotic retail world to the more quiet and laid back service world was like working for two different companies. There was a lot less structure than I was used to. I embraced it because it was calmer than what I'd just left.

For the second time in six months, I was getting to know a whole new group of people.

I had to learn a completely different aspect of the company. Due to my background in operations, I had an inkling of what the service centers did because we processed customer drop-offs and pick-ups.

As a service rep, my job was to answer phones, assist technicians with their paperwork and process products being received from the stores. In comparison to all the different responsibilities I had on the retail side of the business, this was child's play. I learned that while the retail holiday season is between Thanksgiving and Christmas, the repair holiday was from New Year's until almost St. Patrick's Day. I arrived at the center just in time for another busy season. The technicians were about 3-4 weeks backlogged with repairs, which led to angry customers. I worked overtime to find out as much as I could and help in other departments. **That sped up my learning curve and earned me a lot of respect from my co-workers.**

I had forgotten what it felt like to be judged solely on my own personal work. For the previous three years, I had been in positions of authority, where the performance of my subordinates reflected on me. It didn't take long to get comfortable in my new role and location. I received a pay cut in the demotion, but with overtime, my check barely took a hit. Life was good again! And it was at that point (February 1996) I decided that I was done with taking on roles that made me responsible for other people's job performance – well, kind of. At one point in late 1997, I applied for the vacant Operations Manager position in the service center. I rescinded my application a few days later because I realized that although the new gm *Michael and I got along, he appeared to micromanage the assistants. I had left that when I transferred from the store and wasn't willing to go through it again.

*Journal Entry 12/2/98- A few months ago I celebrated my 6th year anniversary with Best Buy. I'm still at the service center and loving it tremendously. My current title is tech admin. I audit tags, research warranty rejections, assist technicians, handle exchange paperwork and solve billing problems. I work 50 to 60 hours a week and love every minute of it. I share an office with two other ladies. They are tech admin also, but they take directions from me. *Michael basically created the position for me based on the tasks I had taken on. I moved from the office to the tech area in May of '97. I basically did what I do now, except I closed the tags too. Plus there were only 30 or so technicians. Around August (of '97), *Marty decided to have a 2nd person in the position to help me out. By May of '98, it was determined that all centers would have tech admin positions, and that we needed 3 people. The Indianapolis & Wisconsin centers had already closed, so those stores' product* *started coming to us, which bring us up to 39 stores.*

REEMERGENCE

From the time that I rescinded my manager application in 1997 until the middle of 1999, the service center had gone through three general managers and two operations managers. In fact, after the last ops manager quit in late 1998, that position stayed vacant until I decided to try again in mid 1999.

I was still quite content in my tech admin role because I really felt like I was making a difference.

Our revenue came from billing the manufacturers and extended warranty companies for repairs. The reimbursement paperwork had to be precise for us to receive payment. Any errors resulted in rejections, which left the technicians and the company unpaid for repairs that had been already completed. Since part of my job as tech admin was to audit the paperwork before we closed the work orders, my role was very integral in making sure we received our revenue. During the time I held that position, we cut rejections in half!

In the meantime, customer service was running amuck. It was rumored that the operations manager position was still open because external candidates thought the pay was too low. Some internal candidates applied, but *Murray, the GM at the time, felt they weren't qualified for the job. After going a few months without filling it , *Murray decided to add two supervisor positions that would report to one of the other managers.

Over my three and a half years there, the number of stores we serviced nearly doubled. As a result, our staff had increased quite a bit. The growing number of technicians, inventory and parts employees made sense due to the larger volume. But I didn't understand why the number of customer service reps had nearly doubled when they had one-third the workload of previous years. They only had to answer phones and take in product at the counter. The inventory receiving process became automated and my tech admin team handled all the paperwork and technician inquiries. Not to mention, childish, unprofessional behavior was allowed by the new supervisors who themselves lacked leadership reexperience. Day after day I witnessed the waste of resources, funds and potential.

I tried to ignore it. But the more I observed the problems, I knew I could solve them, and that "leadership itch" came back. If I became the operations manager, I would be in charge of the department and liable for anything that went wrong. Was I ready to move from the shallow waters of the ocean and try management again? The answer was "YES!"

THE SUBTLE SHARK EMBRACES BEING A LEADER

Subtle Shark Exploration

What aspects of being a leader are you trying to suppress?

What past experiences derailed you from your true calling?

★ ★ ★ ★ ★ ★ ★ ★ ★ ★ ★

About a week or so after submitting my application for the position, we got a new Regional Service Manager, *Ben. So although *Murray had already decided to promote me, *Ben wanted to conduct an interview to make sure I could do the job. I ended up getting it in May 1999 and immediately went to work setting expectations and holding the customer service team accountable to the rules that were already in place, but not being enforced. Within three to four months I ended up with about half the number of people I started with because they either quit or were fired due to policy violations. **I prided myself in managing a small team while ensuring they were trained to help out in other departments when necessary.** I had stopped the waste that was going on, but soon faced different obstacles.

Journal Entry 12/18/99- On the work front, so much is still going on. Between the remodel, the backlog, losing one of my supervisors to another position and everything else, it's been a daily challenge. I've decided that what I can't get done in 8 hours won't get done. The rest of the management team (except one) barely comes to work, so I'm going to just do what I can. It's a challenge to keep the counter guys busy, handle customer issues and decide what to do if she gets this HR position. I admit that between resolving the ton of customer issues and creating new tags to get problem tags shipped back to the stores, I don't really have control of my department. I need to write out an action plan.

*Journal Entry 1/2/00- I decided not to make itemized resolutions this time. I want to be an effective Operations Manager. With the rollout of this new system, I feel as though I've lost my way. I didn't know how to plan for it. But after 2 ½ months, I've got a pretty good grasp. The counter closing down pretty soon will help. I've just got to stop letting customer problems consume me. I just need to talk to *Murray about some issues I need to resolve so that I can make and execute my plans.*

A few months later *Murray was terminated; the third GM in less than three years. *Ben and the new Human Resource Manager, *Shannon met with each assistant individually. They stated that until the backlog was eliminated, we would all have to work open to close and help each other out. I was furious! I continued to lend a hand in other departments when time permitted, but now it was being mandated and I didn't like it one bit.

This was my first dose of colleagues bringing me down.

I had been working extra hours to get customer service under control, with no help from my peers. *Ben's feeling was that we should all be responsible for each other and not be in the "silo" of our own departments. All I could think was that **it took me years to get comfortable with being responsible for the actions of the people in my department. Now I'm responsible for the actions of the managers of other departments.** Although I didn't agree with it at the time & it made me really angry with *Ben, I learned a valuable lesson about true teamwork from the situation. I dug in, helped out where I could and it only took a few weeks to reach the goal.

THE SUBTLE SHARK DOES NOT WORK IN A SILO

Subtle Shark Exploration

What type of relationships do you have with your colleagues?

How are you helping them to become better?

Shortly thereafter, *Murray's replacement, *Marcus came aboard as a transfer from a nearby store. We weren't really sure what to make of him, since this was the first time since *Jane that the GM didn't have a repair background. He seemed like a nice enough person, but we questioned the thought process of bringing him in. By then I had been a part of service for almost twice as long as I had been in retail. Although I appreciated both businesses, I was now officially "Team Service." It probably took close to a year for tensions to ease about *Marcus' motives because he kept transferring retail people in to fill service center positions, including two managers.

I remember when *Marcus was about to bring in the second manager, *Travis, he asked me if I'd be interested in switching to a different department. The thinking was that *Travis' background was customer service, so it would be an easier transition for him, but I wasn't feeling it. Admittedly, I was in selfish mode. Customer service ran smoothly; and I wasn't about to let someone come in and benefit from the fruits of my labor. Secondly, I had just re-enrolled in school, so I didn't want to have to deal with the pressures of running a new department, while taking classes. Thirdly, the other departments were still struggling to get on track, so every time *Ben came in to visit, he gave those managers a hard time. I had finally gotten him off my back, so I didn't want to regress.

Once *Marcus and I got past our growing pains, we developed a great relationship. I was really good at my job, did what he asked and was getting along well with my peers. Because of my experience during my first go round as a manager, I was more outspoken. I'm sure at times that annoyed *Marcus, but ultimately, I think he appreciated knowing exactly where I was coming from. He gave me more responsibilities, which helped build my confidence. Once I earned his trust, he supported me with the other managers and sent them to me for final decisions on fiscal matters. After a while, he counted on me to manage his schedule, and left me in charge of the center when he traveled for work or went on vacation. Because he had shown so much assurance in me and my abilities, I went out of my way to make his job easier by proactively dealing with any issues that arose.

CHAPTER SIX'S

SUBTLE SHARK BITES

How I bounced back from disappointment & flourished:

You may or may not be born a leader, but once you have unleashed those qualities, embrace them

Failure does not define you, trying again is what matters

A management position is not about your department, it's about every department

CHAPTER SEVEN
MIGRATION

Many species of animals migrate for various reasons and sharks are no exception. In most cases, they are required to travel to their food source if it's scarce in their current location. Like it or not, sometimes a change of setting is essential to survive. Because of some changes in the business, I was forced to migrate. I wasn't happy about it, but it was necessary at the time. Fortunately, I was able to come full circle.

OFF COURSE

*Journal Entry 6/3/03- This past Thursday *Shannon & *Marcus sat me down to let me know that the company was combining the Ops & Parts Managers positions. As a result, I no longer had a job at the service center & *Travis would be the manager filling the new position. Needless to say, I was quite stunned because I know that I am a far superior manager than *Travis. I was given the option of going to a store as an Ops or Inventory Manager. There was also a severance package of 11 weeks for my 11 years of service. But they both said they hoped I didn't take it. *Marcus had been looking pretty sick for the last couple of weeks and during our conversation the day before he said that a lot of crap was going to be happening. He also said that he hoped people wouldn't be mad at him as a result. Now it all makes sense. I'm doing okay, considering. All of this seems like an out of body experience. Even as I packed my stuff, it seemed like I was watching it happening, as opposed to it actually happening to me. I just can't see myself going back to a store. But I am very thankful that it was not a termination, so I'll be okay. Too bad I can't say the same for the Service Center. My knowledge far outweighs that of the management team combined and it will be sorely missed. But everything happens for a reason.*

Clearly that entry was filled with a lot of ego – but if you don't think you're the best, who will? When they brought me in to tell me, I honestly didn't see it coming. At first there was stunned silence then I just couldn't stop crying. I was seriously considering taking the severance package, but Diane talked me out of it. Her feeling was that I wasn't prepared to begin a job search after 10 years of being at one company. I know I should have been appreciative that they had alternative positions lined up for me, but I was devastated. I loved my job! And although I enjoyed retail, I was a lot older now and didn't have the same level of energy that was required to work in the store. The following journal entries say it all...

Journal Entry 6/17/03- On Friday I met with the District Manager and District Operations Manager about my store placement @1pm, for them to act like they were going to accommodate me. But I ended up where they originally planned two weeks ago. The only benefit is the shorter distance & absolutely nothing else. I am quite salty.

My experience at the store yesterday was excruciating! Everyone was really nice, which was the only good thing. The store is old and I just have this overwhelming feeling that this is NOT what I'm supposed to be doing. I wish I'd taken the severance package. Yesterday really made me realize that I MUST seek employment elsewhere. Since I have to start over, it may as well be someplace else, eleven years is enough. I believe I've run my course at Best Buy.

*My going away party at 610 was really nice last Tuesday. *Marcus presented the cake & made a little speech. I made one of my own stating that the gifts and acknowledgements are bittersweet because you get this type of thing only when you're leaving. I also thanked everyone for making my job so easy by doing what I asked and helping when I needed it. I told them I felt like the mother hen & I don't think anyone would take care of them like me. But clearly God has something else planned for me & I never would have left on my own. They gave me a huge greeting card and a beautiful plant.*

Journal Entry 6/19/03-It hasn't been a week yet & I am completely worn out. I hung out in customer service and just felt like I was about to explode!!! I just felt so out of place and so like retail wasn't meant for me anymore. I wanted to just bolt out of the store, never to return. I said a prayer for peace & clarity about what I should really do about my situation. Shortly thereafter the GM and I sat down and talked about the circumstances that brought me to the store. He mostly talked about his expectations for the store and the fact that for the amount of experience they have, the Ops department doesn't really work up to their potential. He said that part of the problem with the whole store is that the revolving door of managers keeps things too unstable, so there hasn't been any cohesiveness, plus the supervisors haven't been held accountable. The entire conversations somehow made me feel like I should stick it out (the power of prayer) at least through the holidays.

Journal Entry 6/23/03- I can't wait until my off days this week. Although I no longer want to run out of the store screaming, retail is NOT for me. I may not last until the holidays...

*Journal Entry 6/25/03- *Ben & someone from the district team were doing a store visit when I got there. They came into the office where my trainer & I were doing the schedule. *Ben said I hadn't been keeping in touch and didn't even call to yell at him or anything. I told him I wanted to slap him around & he was more than willing to let me do it. He just kept saying that I didn't know the whole story...whatever that means. I'm excited to be off for the next two days. I'm much more rested since I'm in training mode @ work.*

Journal Entry 7/6/03- After talking to Di, I've decided to go back to my plan C, which is to actively pursue employment elsewhere, while maintaining my current position. It's not horrible, yet isn't what I'm supposed to be doing (retail). But I'll have the option of not just taking the first thing I come across & possibly making much more money, with much better hours.

THE SUBTLE SHARK WORKS THROUGH ADVERSITY

★ ★ ★ ★ ★ ★ ★ ★ ★ ★ ★

Subtle Shark Exploration

What hardships are you currently experiencing in your career or business?

What are you doing to work through any setbacks that arise?

RIDING THE CREST

*Journal Entry 7/11/03- Oh Happy Day!!! Well the rumors are true, apparently *Travis is becoming a GM at a service center on the East Coast. I can't wait!!! I've got to get out of retail...I'm just not cut out for that type of work anymore. I bet I'll take the severance package the next time.*

Journal Entry 8/2/03- Today is the beginning of the rest of my life. This is my last shift at the store and although the people were great, I'm glad to be going back to 610. I'm looking forward to the challenge of learning the Parts Department and getting the operations supervisor ready to fill my shoes. It's also going to be a real challenge keeping "the boys" in line, all while going back to school.

I was ecstatic to be back at home, but harbored resentment against *Marcus. I was probably snippy with him for a few months. To be honest, I didn't even realize the root-cause until we finally talked it out. From that point on, our relationship went back to where it was before all the craziness ensued.

Tension built amongst the assistant managers due to disagreements about everyone doing their fair share. I found myself in the middle of a lot of pettiness and in-fighting. What I observed was just egos getting in the way. I got along pretty well with my peers, which is why they came to me to complain about each other. **Whether I agreed or not, I really tried to give them another point of view or a less confrontational way to handle the situation instead of fanning the flame.** It worked when they listened and took my advice.

Some challenges presented themselves with my new department. It was a lot like the management team as far as the in-fighting, but the twist was that most of the team didn't respect the supervisor. **This was one of the first times I worked to actively help someone develop their leadership skills.** It was an uphill battle which tested my patience. The experience benefited me as I worked on completing my degree in Management. I wrote many a paper about leadership and employee behavior by the time I graduated, and all of it was based on real observations, not theory.

In late 2004, our center took on a major repair initiative. It meant increasing our staff (including two additional managers) and adding a second shift to work in the evenings. Again there were management personality conflicts and the second shift felt second class. It was difficult managing employees from my department that worked on two different shifts consistently. But I ended up pulling from my retail experience to get through it. There was a lot of finger pointing in the beginning as employees on different shifts complained about one another's work. But I tried to nip that in the bud quickly. **I encouraged them to give constructive feedback and ask questions to gain more clarity, instead of automatically jumping to conclusions.**

Our location did so well with the repair initiative that it led to the company taking it to a much larger scale and building a "super service center" in Kentucky in 2006. And while it was great that we were able to prove that such a project would be successful and add hundreds of jobs to the company, it meant that many people would lose their jobs in our service center. *Marcus got the facility manager position early in the year. By late March, the assistant manager positions were posted for the new location so I applied. I had every intention of applying to fill *Marcus' vacated position, but I wanted to hedge my bets in case I didn't get the promotion. Whereas I felt capable of taking over as General Manager, there was still an interview process and I didn't know what type of experience my competition would bring to the table.

THE SUBTLE SHARK KEEPS MOVING FORWARD

★ ★ ★ ★ ★ ★ ★ ★ ★ ★ ★

Subtle Shark Exploration

Are you dwelling on past adversities or are you focused on the future?

How can you take all the experience you've gained so far and turn it into new opportunities?

★ ★ ★ ★ ★ ★ ★ ★ ★ ★ ★

There were two panel interviews for the assistant manager job. Everyone knew that I applied for the GM position and during the second panel, *Marcus asked me straight out which one I'd prefer. The question caught me off guard, but it wasn't like I hadn't thought about it. Relocating to Kentucky offered some unique benefits and future opportunities for promotion. I'd always wanted to be in on the ground floor of a location where I could be part of determining the structure and hiring my own people. But who in their right mind would turn down the chance to run their own market? This would be my biggest career jump since I went from supervisor to manager ten years earlier.

However, this time it felt right. I had worked closely with *Marcus for the past couple of years, so I had learned a lot, especially about the "people" aspect of being a leader. Sure there were going to be some obstacles, but I grew up in this location and it didn't need "fixing," it needed nurturing. I could handle that.

I got the promotion! I was now responsible for the Chicago Service Center and In-Home Markets and the Detroit In-Home Market. One of the assistant managers transferred to Kentucky and within a few months, one of the other managers quit. I didn't replace them. I was left with six managers who reported to me and about 150 employees across Illinois, Indiana and Michigan, which was manageable.

CHAPTER SEVEN'S

SUBTLE SHARK BITES

To build solid relationships and a quality reputation:

Become invaluable to your team

Keep your boss informed of what you are doing

Remove the ego when dealing with conflict

CHAPTER EIGHT
IN THE DEEP

Sharks' skeletons are made of cartilage, which is more flexible and lighter than bone. It gives them the speed to be powerful predators. A shark's shape is designed to navigate long distances and maneuver easily around its prey. I had spent the past 13 years hunting with the occasional "hit and runs" and "bump and bites". I was nimble and had dug in deep, surviving the tides, veering off and back on course, feeding on knowledge and attacking experience. Now I was prepared for my biggest promotion and responsibility to date. Some species of sharks can have up to eight fins, which are used to stabilize, lift and move them forward. My fins are my leadership skills. I had honed and used them to get where I was, but needed them in high gear to handle the massive waves ahead of me in this larger ocean.

THE TIDAL WAVE

I hit the ground running once I was officially named General Manager of the service center in May 2006. Immediately I was booked on a flight to St. Louis for an annual meeting that all GMs were required to attend. I made the announcement on Monday morning to the service center that I was their location manager, and then headed to the airport. During the trip I met the other ten service center GMs who all lived in different parts of the country.

When I got back from St. Louis, I went through a few weeks of training with my counterpart from Denver. Next was the staff reduction, then our relocation to a new building. The week of the move, I was out of town. **I had to trust my managers to carry out our plan without my direct supervision.** Everything went off without a hitch.

My new boss *Robert visited a few times to follow up. One of the most important things he told me was now that I was the GM, I'm ALWAYS on stage. Although I worked with the majority of my employees for almost 10 years and as a manager over half that time, things were different now that I was responsible for the entire location. I thought maybe he was exaggerating, but I took heed. The first thing I started doing was dressing up, instead of wearing a uniform.

I did it as a constant reminder that I had to carry myself a little differently now.

I maintained the balance of being easy-going yet getting the job done; qualities I admired in some of my favorite managers over the years. But now every conversation and observation had a big picture focus and changed my perspective.

A few months into my new position, I was out of town with my fellow GMs. During a chat with two of them after hours, they expressed concern that I was so quiet during our business meetings. What they didn't understand is that I was in learning mode. It was our first time meeting in that capacity, so **I was observing the group dynamics and understanding where I could add value.** Additionally, I've never been a "say something just to be part of the conversation" type of person. I assured them that being less talkative doesn't mean I can't hold my own. During that discussion, I gleaned another piece of advice from *Monty. He said that he may not know all of the statistics on the scorecard, but he knows all of his employees' birthdays and how many kids they have. That was the first time I'd heard someone say **"take care of your employees and they'll take care of you"** and really mean it that deeply.   In my mind *Monty became my unofficial mentor from that point on. I had always believed in and tried to practice building good relationships with employees, but he inspired me to take it to another level.

During one of my business trips, *Robert's boss, *Martin (yep, my former store manager) conducted what he referred to as a "Skip Level" with the GMs. He called it that because he was skipping a level of direct-reporting by meeting with his subordinate's subordinates. The purpose was to give us an opportunity to speak candidly about any issues we were facing overall or with *Robert.

THE SUBTLE SHARK SEES THE BIG PICTURE

Subtle Shark Exploration

What mundane details are occupying the majority of your time?

What is your long-term vision for your career or business?

Within the next 60 days, I decided to have "Roundtable Discussions" with all of my employees using *Martin's method. Although I felt that my locations didn't need "fixing," there was room for improvement. I created a safe environment for employees to voice concerns, as well as action items for myself to focus on for the next year. In small groups they had the chance to verbalize their thoughts, as well as write them down, in case they wanted to retain a little bit of anonymity. I used the feedback to set expectations during manager meetings. It was a pretty time consuming process, but worth every minute. While it was somewhat difficult to address every single issue brought to light, I did the best I could. And even though I may have fallen short sometimes with swift resolutions to work-related problems, there's no doubt in my mind that I was actively earning the trust of many employees. No matter what else was going on, I knew I was doing my job well when individuals would come to me about extremely private matters. **In most cases, they knew I couldn't help them directly, but they needed someone to talk to so they confided in me.**

I started quarterly one-on-ones with the 12 supervisors and team leads. The purpose was three-fold: Get to know each of them individually, validate what the assistant managers told me and give them the opportunity to voice their concerns. I gained tons of valuable insight that helped me make better decisions over the years.

Less than a year after my promotion, in early 2007, *Robert took another position and *Ben became my new "old" boss. I had just gotten adjusted to *Robert's management style, so when I first found out he was changing jobs, I was concerned. But, once I learned *Ben would be his replacement I was excited because I knew his method all too well. He wasn't one of my favorite people when he first came along, but over the years we developed an understanding. Do your job, do it well and he'll let you be. I felt like I was in a good place. The service center was running well, so I focused a lot of my attention on learning the in-home repair business. As Operations Manager, I had nothing to do with In Home and didn't seek to learn it when it came under *Marcus' purview a few months prior. It seemed overly complicated to me and the more I learned about it, the more I realized I was right. But if understanding In Home was the biggest hurdle I was going to face in my new position, it wasn't going to be a problem. My first year as GM had been pretty busy with my training and travel, a major staff reduction, the service center relocation and implementing a culture of consistent employee engagement. **Yet I got through it successfully because I was allowed to run my business, connect more deeply with my employees and receive guidance as needed.** With as much as I had conquered, little did I know that my first year would be the easiest.

THE TSUNAMI

In April 2007 I learned that some smaller service centers would be turned into cross-docks. They would repair only large items, while the smaller products were shipped to the larger centers. As a result, these locations would be experiencing staff reductions. There were a few caveats to me finding out this information when I did. The official announcements weren't being made for at least another 60 days, so not even the other GMs knew yet. I was being told because the GM of one of the soon-to-be affected locations was transferring and they of course wouldn't be backfilling the position. So I was going to be the interim GM until after the announcement was made and the transition took place. Although I figured part of the reason I was chosen was because logistically I was the closest, **I was still honored that I was trusted with such a huge undertaking when I hadn't yet completed my rookie year.** At the same time it was one of the most stressful experiences of my life. I was going to spend the next few months getting to know people that would be losing their jobs and I had to act like everything was okay. On top of that, I couldn't even talk to my peers about it because they weren't informed and some would be affected. This would be my second big layoff in less than two years.

Journal Entry 4/21/07- I spent this week in St Louis, which was very interesting. The GM (soon to be leaving) gave me a tour of the center and introduced me to everyone. They were very cordial and welcoming. I spent the rest of the week getting to know, the Ops/Parts/Inv manager. She's seems really nice and competent, but she's still green because she's only been in the role for about 9 months. She definitely has her work cut out for her, but I was able to help her prioritize and let her know what I want her to focus on for the next week. On Thursday I attended their weekly leadership meeting and was able to talk to the two leads about how I manage and what my expectations are. I had to lie and tell them that I didn't know whether or not the center would be closing. But I did let them know that I would be managing St Louis as if it were staying open forever although we never know the fate of any service center. I do feel really stressed building relationships with these people, knowing the dismal fate of the center. I'm hoping that there will be opportunities for everyone and that they won't be too upset with me when it's all said and done. I know it's a part of the job, but that doesn't make it any easier.

So I take on another service center in which the two Assistant Managers have been in their positions for less than a year <u>and</u> we have to fix the worst inventory debacle I have EVER seen! We had to bring in Inventory Supervisors from other locations to help with the research. Although I had never been an Inventory Manager, I always helped with the counts and reconciliations every year. That experience really paid off. My schedule for the next five months was to spend the first half of each week in Chicago and the second half in St. Louis. I racked up many frequent flyer miles!

The layoffs a few months later were painful, but we made it through. Not even a year later, just when everything had finally settled down and my travel schedule had eased, we went through ANOTHER service center dust up where a few more service centers were converted to crossdocks.

*Journal entry 3/9/08- *Ben informed me on Friday that I will be taking on even more responsibility with the upcoming transitions. I will be adding the Cleveland crossdock and In Home to my realm of influence. I always welcome more responsibility. My only concern is that they rarely meet budget, so I'm going to have to figure out why. Part of me feels that if current management hasn't figured it out, then how can I? But the more confident/optimistic part of me feels that I have a special knack for this type of stuff, which is why I've been successful in the past. I'm excited about the prospect and also need to get a travel plan together, since now I will be responsible for 3 remote locations.*

THE SUBTLE SHARK ALWAYS TAKES ON NEW CHALLENGES

Subtle Shark Exploration

What challenges have you shunned in order to stay in your comfort zone?

How quickly do you tackle new challenges so that you are ready for the next?

★ ★ ★ ★ ★ ★ ★ ★ ★ ★ ★

So here we go, my third layoff in as many years. It is emotionally exhausting delivering such devastating news to people while trying to remain professional. I was up to the challenge of taking on more, still I absolutely hated having to tell yet another group of people that they were losing their jobs. This new responsibility was coupled with the fact that the GM of the Cleveland locations, who up until this point was my peer, would now be my direct-report. We had always gotten along, so I wasn't concerned about that, but I was going to need to balance the dynamics that come with her basically doing the same job, but it actually being a lesser role. We talked candidly about everything. She very easily and readily accepted me as her new boss and I let her know about my leadership style and expectations. Her experience as GM made her extremely easy to manage, plus I valued and sought her expertise regularly.

I spent the next year getting to know the remaining Cleveland employees and pushing my growing management team to work together and get out of their silos. **As part of my overall development, *Ben put me on corporate work teams and partnered me with a mentor (director-level) to increase my knowledge and sphere of influence.** I regularly traveled to the corporate office for meetings, contributed to new initiatives and built relationships with the team members. Additionally, I focused on partnering more with my retail counterparts to educate them on repairs. There had always been a love/hate relationship between our parts of the business. Most misunderstandings were based on poor communication or lack of understanding. I worked really hard with them to bridge that gap by offering regularly scheduled educational visits. The added bonus was that my employees spearheaded this initiative, which gave them a sense of empowerment and ownership.

Like clockwork, less than a year after the Cleveland transition, we went through another big change…*Ben's position was eliminated. I was really concerned because he had always been an advocate for me, took an active role in my development, got on my case when needed, and let me do my own thing when I earned it. I really liked working for him this time around and now I would have my third new boss in less than three years.

*Journal Entry 3/1/09- I talked to *Ben at length on Tuesday evening for the first time since it was announced that his position was being eliminated. He said that he applied for several other positions and is determined to stay with the company. He spent the majority of the phone call coaching me on everything from updating my resume and JOS profile to making sure my team hits the ground running. He kept saying there's no "whining" in Services. Of course I'm a little concerned about getting a new boss. *Ben has been one of the biggest advocates for Chicago. *Ben's other advice to me was to network! Network! Network! I think that will be my biggest challenge. I just have to work hard to produce the results. My managers had better be prepared to see a less patient Ayesha. I'm not taking any more steps backward to move forward. So I can't allow anyone to get in the way, including people who don't embrace change and are stuck in the old way of thinking.*

THE SUBTLE SHARK EXPANDS THE SPHERE OF INFLUENCE

Subtle Shark Exploration

Who is a part of your professional network?

How do you provide value to their career or business & how do they do the same for you?

*Journal Entry 4/26/09- The trip to Louisville went pretty well. Nothing earth shattering was revealed. We just gained some clarity around *Nick's (*Ben's replacement) perspective and expectations. He seems open-minded, but has some very strong thoughts and opinions around what should be done. He stated several times that he's not going to micromanage us and that he trusts us to run our own businesses. He has cautioned us to make sure we are controlling expenses and not making decisions that will put our employees in "harm's way". What has really resonated with me is the fact that he wants to "remove the noise" from the system for us so that we can remain focused. Though I love the relationship I've built with the corporate parts team, I think I can still maintain it even with a change in my link role. I got a chance to spend some 1:1 time with *Nick on the way to the airport. I let him know I was excited about the direction we're going and even possibly naively optimistic. He let me know that he's straight forward and doesn't beat around the bush.*

*Journal Entry 5/17/09- The Tuesday before last I had my annual performance appraisal discussion w/*Ben & HR on a conference call. I was very disappointed in my overall score of 2.8 (values 3.1) which are my lowest scores in the history of my career at BBY. I know In Home negatively affected everyone's business scores. The feedback I got is that teaching the values is the expectation with my direct-reports and subordinates. To be above expectations I have to teach them with my peers and others outside my direct sphere of influence. I just wish I'd known that before my review. Of course I still need to calibrate w/*Nick to find out what his expectations are, but I heard the message loud and clear.*

The first year under *Nick wasn't bad. He was getting to know all of us and setting expectations for the business. He was a pretty straight shooter, even though sometimes he would metaphor me to death when trying to explain things. **The biggest focus was for the GMs**

to work more as a team and share best practices with each other. Although I had developed really good relationships with my peers over the previous few years, there was still work to be done. We usually all got together for business meetings every couple of months. I tried to expand upon it by calling each of them every couple of weeks.

*Journal Entry 2/14/10- I was a little stressed out at the beginning of last week in anticipation of my monthly 1:1 with *Nick. I thought he was going to "dwell on" or "beat me up" over Chicago's turn time, which is 4-5 days higher than most other centers. A couple of GMs had each called me to let me know that *Nick had been asking them about it. Thanks to them, I had continued to dig in even more than I had been before. And due to that I had answers and a plan for why and how to fix the problems. So overall, my 1:1 ended up not being bad at all.*

*Journal Entry 2/28/10- Our Viewpoint scores came out on Thursday and I was very excited to see that the Great Lakes overall engagement went up to 4.15 from 4.04 and overall satisfaction stayed the same at 4.24. The other thing I'm proud of is that my high scores tied only w/*Monty when no other GMs had both scores over a 4. Yahoo!!!*

Journal Entry 5/9/10- The previous week wasn't much to speak of anyway. It started off w/my annual performance appraisal. My score was a 3 which is meets expectations, which was not much of a surprise. Nick's biggest feedback was that I am too easy on my assistant mangers. His words were that I need to let them succeed or fail on their own. I've already got my game plan together so that I'm in contention for an "above expectations" this year.

I continued to work on my development by signing up for leadership training courses that were being offered at the corporate office and continuing to talk to my mentor on a monthly basis. At this point, the number of stores I serviced and the number of employees I was responsible for had more than doubled, so I had my hands full.

I learned so much from the training courses, I decided to pay it forward to my employees. Although the company offered management training to supervisor level and above, it was always so retail focused that service center employees didn't really get a lot out of it. Besides, I felt there was more of a need for "leadership" training, which is very different than "management." So in 2009, I created a mandatory leadership training curriculum for all of the supervisors and team leads that reported to me. Shortly thereafter, I created a leadership training course for the line level employees on my teams because there was no company offered opportunities for them. It was voluntary, but I had ground rules, pre-work and post-work to be completed, to ensure active participation. Preparing for and facilitating the classes was also another form of learning for me.

THE SUBTLE SHARK SHARES KNOWLEDGE

★ ★ ★ ★ ★ ★ ★ ★ ★ ★ ★

Subtle Shark Exploration

What are you doing to continue your professional development?

How are you helping others to improve their skills?

*Journal Entry 5/30/10- Wednesday & Thursday were brutal due to my visit from *Nick, *Gene, and the support manager. I was unsure of the purpose of the visit, especially this soon after *Nick was just here last month. He stated that the visit was to set expectations. Last year we focused on behaviors, this year it will be about digging into the business and delivering results. They let us know what they'll be looking at and looking for in future visits and how we should prepare. I got a lot of constructive feedback on my management team and they were only impressed with one of my managers. I'm disappointed in myself because I knew what needed to be done and had been focusing on so many other things that I hadn't truly been holding my management team accountable the way I should. I fuss a lot when things aren't done correctly, but there are no true repercussions. And that's where I failed them and I failed myself, so I need to correct that and see who the cream that will rise to the top is. *Gene stressed to me that I need to get it done my way and that it doesn't necessarily require me walking around with a big stick, if that's not my style. I had things on my calendar that I keep moving or deleting for other priorities. They didn't tell me much that I didn't already know, which is embarrassing to me because we should have been doing it. So the visit was a mental beat down for me because it brought to light all of my deficiencies. But the team was very respectful, constructive and candid in their feedback*

and expectations.

The second year under *Nick wasn't great. We never clashed, but we never really "got" each other either. When I complained about it to Diane, she advised, "Your job is to understand your boss and do what he says. Don't worry about if he understands you or not." I didn't approach my employees in this way, but I thought maybe she had a point. He was just a few years older than me, but he had an "old school" approach.

My style of leadership clashed with his direction for the team. From my perspective, it was this vicious cycle of him telling me his opinion of what is wrong then saying, "I'm not going to tell you *how* to handle it," or "you aren't meeting expectations" after I thought I'd handled it. I just kept making adjustments the best way I saw fit.

Of my fellow GMs, I probably talked to *Stewart the most during this time yet, he was my EXACT opposite personality-wise. I was very deliberative in my thought patterns and very cautious in my approach. He was always two or three steps ahead in his mind and thrived off of stirring things up. Not only did we respect each other's differences, but we sought advice with situations that played to the other person's strengths. *Stewart's qualities were the most like *Nick's on our team, so I often asked *Stewart for advice when I needed help dealing with our boss. I knew I would never be like *Stewart, which wasn't my goal anyway, but I appreciated his insights because I tried to see where it overlapped with my approach, so that I could meld the two and attempt to meet *Nick's expectations. Sometimes it worked. Most of the time it didn't.

Journal Entry 3/13/11- December and January were rough because we found out we were closing all the crossdocks and weren't announcing it for another three weeks. It was stressful but went as well as could be expected. I wasn't able to prepare for the new year (calendar & fiscal) like I normally prefer to do because of my continued travel schedule, so technically my new year starts today. I only had one month free of traveling, so I was back on the grid this past Thursday with a trip to Cleveland. They are on pace to finish everything before April 8th and spirits are as to be expected, but they were nice to me.

Here we go again, another layoff! I went almost two years without one.

As with all of the other business transitions, I ended up with more responsibility.

I gained another assistant manager and two more markets. My hands were full with the performance management of a few of my current direct-reports, and it was about to increase by one. My new manager struggled with integrity, communication and follow up. With the business shift, he gained an additional market, thus two team leads and did not handle it well. To make a long story short, because of the immediate crisis he caused, I quickly identified where I needed to focus when it came to his performance management.

It was important to make sure the new members of my team felt a part of the family. Now I had 19 in home team leads in at least seven different states that may have talked on the phone, but had never met one another. Their idea was to have a Great Lakes In-Home Summit. They created an agenda, met in Chicago, developed a plan to move forward and felt more connected as a result.

My responsibilities had almost quadrupled over the five years after I was promoted to General Manager. I faced each new challenge with zeal and never lost sight of the fact that my employees were my most valuable resource.   But after more than a year of feeling beat down with no end in sight, something had to give (details are in the next book of this series). So in December of 2011, I decided to end my journey at Best Buy, just shy of my 20-year anniversary. The choice was bittersweet because I had learned so much and built so many great relationships, but I knew it was the right thing for me. I have not looked back and have not had one ounce of regret. It was time for permanent migration.

CHAPTER EIGHT'S

SUBTLE SHARK BITES

LESSONS FROM THE MOST STRESSFUL AND REWARDING POSITION

I HAD EVER HELD:

The higher your position:

1. **the more secrets you must keep about things you don't want to know**
2. **the more you must expand your sphere of influence**
3. **the greater your obligation to be of service to your employees**
4. **the more important it is to genuinely interact with those in lower positions**

The higher your position, the more essential it is for your reports to trust in you

BONUS CHAPTERS

CHAPTER 9
PREDATORS

Their skin is rough as a means of protection, but there are very few natural predators of sharks; only humans, whales and larger sharks. As a result, they're more concerned with hunting for food than defending themselves. Natural predators of the Subtle Shark would be bad bosses, bad colleagues and bad employees.

I am proud of my career achievements and I am equally satisfied with <u>how</u> I went about it. Over the years I encountered people – who whether on purpose or not, endangered my professional journey. Fortunately, due to my natural disposition and focus on the long-term, I fended them off. Anytime I identified potential attacks on me, I concerned myself less with the predator and more with my objectives. This does not mean that I completely ignored them. That would be like a shark simply turning its back to an oncoming attack, which is foolish. But I used my intelligence and skill to disarm them, rendering their threat inconsequential. It wasn't always easy, but it was effective.

BOSS ENCOUNTERS

No matter the job, just about everyone has a boss, and that's where I'll begin. I really learned what a bad boss was during my first few years at Best Buy.

*Journal entry 5/16/93- The more I'm around her the more I'm beginning to hate *Tomasina. I think the major cause stems from a lack of respect. Because I despise her jealousy and backstabbing, it makes it hard for me to tolerate her presence. We had an extremely irrelevant meeting yesterday that didn't get anything accomplished. She just talked about what she didn't*

see getting done. She hasn't seen anything because she hasn't been around.

It wasn't just me that had a problem with the condition of customer service. At one point, while *Vanessa was on vacation, I talked to the Inventory Manager, *James about the growing unrest in CS when it comes to *Tomasina. The next day *Beau came to me and asked my opinion about the department's morale. We discussed it at length and he seemed to understand my observations. Within the next few days, *Beau had a talk with *Tomasina and her attitude was much better. She didn't seem bitter. As a matter of fact, she was nice and helpful. But it didn't last for long.

*Journal Entry 8/19/93- Unfortunately *Tomasina is back from her sick leave and is already causing trouble. Right now she's pitting two CSR2s against each other since they both want the senior position. I've been talking to both of them, hoping to prevent a conflict. Yesterday we found out at 4:30pm that *Paul & *Janice were coming in this morning to do their respective audits. *Tomasina's defeatist attitude led her to assume that we'd flunk. So she left. I was angry that she chose the coward's way out. And I was also angry at the prospect of all of my hard work going down the drain. But the other seniors came in for a few hours on their off day to make sure things were in order. The CSR2s stayed late to clean up; and the CSR1s stayed later to assure that I had coverage. Of course we passed, as I knew we would. After this little incident, I've changed my mind about not going to Sunday's roundtable. I'm going to voice my opinion and get some stuff off of my chest.*

For the next few months, things stayed about the same with *Tomasina running the department. Once I decided to concentrate on the things I could control, I felt better. I really liked my job and most of my co-workers, so I focused on the positives. The biggest lesson I learned from the whole *Tomasina experience was to not let others' negativity bring me down. Being so focused on her shortcomings actually made me lose focus on being a better Ayesha.

I was motivated to make the department better, despite her lack of leadership. I just went about it the wrong way.

Over a 19-year career, it stands to reason that I've had a few run-ins with bad bosses and learned a lot from each circumstance. There are tons of one-off situations that I could mention, but that's another book in itself. I'll focus on the most difficult bad boss encounters I had to face over the course of my career.

The Boss Who Is Not Self Aware - He was big on being an inspiring leader and expected the same from his direct-reports. But he was the exact opposite. Anytime he addressed my employees, they walked away discouraged while he seemed excited about the interaction. It's a difficult situation if the boss never asks for or acts on feedback. My suggestion is to offer it anyway. It should be constructive and based on supporting facts. Be careful not to do it in a public setting because the goal is not to embarrass anyone. As with any opinions, a good approach is to begin with the positives. Then when addressing the negatives, offer suggestions on what would make it better in the future. When handled with sincerity and respect the boss may be more open to making adjustments. It's okay if they don't seem receptive initially. The important thing is to at least offer the information. It's up to the boss to decide how to use it.

The Boss with Moving Expectations- This was one of my most frustrating situations.   During a one-on-one he told me I wasn't meeting expectations in a particular aspect of my job. So I asked him what behaviors I would need to exhibit to meet or exceed expectations. Surprisingly, he said to me that he couldn't tell me exactly because they may change in the future. I asked follow-up questions to get him to give some feedback I could use, but to no avail. From there, I talked to my peers to find out how they were doing. A couple of them were meeting his expectations, so we discussed their actions. I modeled some of those behaviors and it actually worked... that is, until the boss changed the expectations again. Then it was back to the drawing board.

The Boss Who Instantly Goes into Panic Mode- Every big issue was a catastrophe. He even once mentioned to me that I never seem to panic, and I told him that panicking never does any good. From then on, he continually questioned my "sense of urgency" when handling issues, even though I always made sure they were resolved. Those conversations were aggravating initially, but I stood my ground and handled things calmly. It didn't stop him from being frenzied when the situations occurred, but I worked on what I could control.

The Boss Who Focuses on the Negative- This boss would basically mention the achievements in passing, then drill incessantly on the issues. I'm not saying that problems don't require attention. But if your employees feel like they're not doing anything right, how will they ever have the confidence to improve. It didn't stop me from sharing my successes with him. He still did not give them as much attention as the failures. However, I felt better having brought it up.

There usually isn't an easy way to deal with a bad boss because they're in charge, right? Some managers are genuine in asking for employee feedback of their performance. If you ever get the opportunity to provide it, do so! Usually if you've built up a significant amount of trust with your superior, it's a lot easier to give them your opinion. Aside from my situation with *Tomasina, I've never gone over my bosses' head to express concern. Yet, it was a very effective method in that instance. I've learned that speaking up is essential, you just have to weigh your fear of possible retaliation (whether real or perceived) against being unhappy 40 hours per week.

COLLEAGUE ENCOUNTERS

Bad colleagues are like family members that you just do not get along with. You can't help who you're related to or who you have to work with. The good thing is you do have some control over how you allow them to treat you and how you react to their behavior. The bad co-workers I've encountered fit into two main categories: lack of work ethic and feeling jealous/threatened.

Lack of Work Ethic

We've all encountered those people who never seem to pull their own weight even at the most basic level. I've grown to understand that everyone is not going to go above and beyond just because that's how I approach things. Yet, I have no patience for those who do the bare minimum. A few years ago, one of my colleagues told me "You can fool your boss, but you can't fool your co-workers." Truer words have never been spoken. The manager can't be everywhere and see everything all the time. Unfortunately, a few employees take advantage of that fact.

Some people's first instinct is to report the co-worker to the boss, which is always a viable solution. Remember that human resource procedures must be followed when it comes to recourse, which can take some time. Meanwhile, you're stuck working next to someone who doesn't seem to care about their job. The thing I learned when dealing with lazy co-workers is not to let them distract me. I was on a trajectory to keep advancing my career and being consumed by their performance wasn't going to help me achieve my goals. Now if their poor behavior directly affected my performance, then instead of digging my heels in or magnifying the conflict, I actually befriended the person. I made sure that the two of us had a good working relationship, that way when I needed something from them, I would ask and they would deliver. This didn't change the fact that they were lazy the rest of the time, but I got what I needed and my job performance wasn't at risk. So many people get caught up in what others aren't doing and even lower their own performance to match. But you are really only hurting yourself whether it's with future career opportunities or more importantly, integrity.

Feeling Jealous/Threatened

Journal Entry 11/17/94- I'm 85% ready to go back home. I liked the experience of coming out here to California. But I'd rather forget the experience of this O-Team. Most of the people were a pleasure training and working with, but most of the sups and mangers were a pain in the butt; especially in Operations. The sup basically refused help. It was frustrating and annoying. The main thing that bothered me about her was that it put her seniors in a bind. They barely got a chance to learn any solid information. We worked a lot of hours, but not much worse than usual. I'll be the first to admit that I've worked harder. But the bad attitudes made me want to rush to get away from that store.

The above entry is referring to my first and last Best Buy Opening Team (O-Team). Whenever new stores opened, experienced employees from other locations helped set up and trained new staff. I wanted to contribute, considering I had learned so much over the previous couple of years. I remembered how daunting it was when our store actually opened. We had been through a month of simulated training, but nothing could prepare us for the spectacle of it all. I was stunned at how uncooperative the new store's supervisor was. The entire time she acted as though she felt threatened by our knowledge, so she wouldn't let us help.

The night of the store's grand opening, the other O-Team supervisor and I tried to help the department with the closing procedures. The local sup told us that she didn't need our assistance. So we left without telling our O-Team manager. When he got back to the hotel, he reamed us for not completing our job, even after we explained what happened. His reasoning was that they didn't know what was good for them and we were there to help, so we should have insisted or got him involved. Honestly, the only lesson I learned from that situation was that we should have reported to our boss before we left. **To this day, I still don't waste my time trying to help people who downright refuse it.**

I have always tried to remain professional, but it did not stop the rumor mill, or those who just had something against me. One person always tried to cause friction for years. In most cases I ignored it because we never worked in the same departments and our jobs didn't overlap. At one point I applied for a position that would make me her boss. One day while chatting with another co-worker, he said, "I didn't know you and *Alana didn't get along." I responded, "As far as I'm concerned, we get along fine because I don't even deal with her. But what would make you say that?" He then told me that she was pretty upset when she found out I applied for the position and was going around telling anyone who would listen that we weren't going to be able to work together. I was so tickled by the situation because to me, she was terrified at the thought that I would retaliate for all the drama she attempted to cause. *Alana soon found out that I had never been that type of person and wasn't going to start. Months, maybe even a year later, when she felt comfortable with me being her boss, she actually admitted to me how upset she was when I applied. She said she was so displeased that she went to the location manager to tell him that we wouldn't get along if he put me in that position. According to her, his response was that she and I were both adults and he trusted that we'd work through it. Imagine that! Unfortunately she hadn't fully learned her lesson because a couple of years later she ended up being terminated for fraudulent behavior that I actually stumbled upon by accident. Although I had let bygones be bygones, apparently karma hadn't.

EMPLOYEE ENCOUNTERS

*Journal Entry 3/26/95- On the work front, *Taylor is losing the little bit of sense she had tucked away. For some reason she's attacking me, which normally I'd be able to handle, except she's playing dirty. Her latest is trying to get everyone to believe that I'm racist & that I show favoritism. She brought it to the Operations Manager, who took it to *Norm, who brought it to my attention. *Norm just basically told me to watch my back with her. I* *would have left it alone, but then I found out she's been making the white ladies in the department feel like I had something against them & that myself and the senior team aren't getting along. The more I talked to people, the more I found out what she's been up to. But I was advised just to document her behavior and leave the slander alone for now. Other than that, everything else is going damn near perfect at work. *Jane did our evaluation Thursday and we got a 96%.*

When I first contemplated career growth in my first couple of years at Best Buy, my ideal situation was to get promoted to a new store. Among other things, it would give me the opportunity to start with a clean slate by staffing my own department. As it turns out, I never got that chance. With every promotion, I inherited the workforce that invariably contained individuals I probably would not have hired myself. *Taylor from the journal entry above was definitely one of those people.

I was still a senior when she was hired and had no input in those decisions at that time. I don't know how she did during the interview process. But, *Taylor had an attitude problem from the start and it never really got any better. I was one of the few people who didn't let her get away with this behavior. She was at odds with everyone in the department all the time. Surprisingly, she never received any customer complaints and did the rest of her job just fine.

After I became the department supervisor, she applied to fill my vacated position as senior. My manager and I conducted the interview and the three of us sat in a semi-circle. *Taylor had the audacity to sit with her chair facing him, almost with her back to me! And even when I asked her questions, she directed her answers to him. In addition, her responses were subpar and she didn't get the position.

Unfortunately, about a year later, the job was open again and qualified candidates were non-existent. My manager and I reluctantly made the decision to give her the promotion. Boy did I regret that! *Taylor challenged me at every turn and annoyed all of the customer service representatives. I continually held her accountable every time I learned of or witnessed an incident. Guess what lesson I learned from that … **It's better to leave a position open than to fill it with someone who is not qualified!**

There are occasions when some people just aren't cut out for the job. Either they never had the skill set to begin with or the job has morphed into something that no longer matches their capabilities. I don't really consider them bad employees, but they must still be addressed.

I always start with training and coaching. Sometimes people simply don't know what to do. If they're willing to learn, why not let them? If the coaching doesn't work, then I help them find a more suitable position if possible. I've had to demote a few employees over the years. Termination should really be a last resort in such situations. **It's trickier when the employee won't admit that they're struggling or if they refuse help.** That's when the kid-gloves come off and you give them some very specific expectations and options. All of the above have worked for me in one situation or another.

BONUS CHAPTERS

CHAPTER TEN
SUBTLE SHARK CHUM

For those of you who don't know, chum is ground fish tidbits used for bait, and that is what this chapter contains. I have hundreds of stories that have contributed to my professional skills and success, but it's too much for one book. I would be remiss if I didn't at least touch on a few more here. This bonus chapter will rundown several key tips that I feel are crucial to any aspiring shark.

KNOW YOURSELF

Be realistic about what you are capable of doing. Do not go after the promotion just because it comes with a pay raise. If the job requires 85% paperwork, but you enjoy spending your work day interacting with others, you will be miserable in that position. Many people knowingly take jobs that don't fit their skill set and interests. They probably convince themselves that it's good money, or that they will find something else in a few months. That good money does not mean as much when you're stuck 40 hours per week doing something you hate. Those few months turn into a few decades when you get too comfortable or too scared to look for better opportunities.

HAVE A PLAN

Once you know what you are capable of doing, create a plan to go after your aspirations. You don't have to know exactly what steps to take because that will come once you know where you are going. It will help you identify which jobs to seek that will get you one step closer to your next goal. It will also help you determine if you should go into business right now or look for a new job. With a plan, you will be less likely to take on something that will actually lead you off your path. You will be surprised how many opportunities appear once you are clear on what you want to accomplish.

GET A MENTOR

Don't waste your time trying to reinvent the wheel. There may be people in your circle, whose opinion you respect that have already been down the road you are about to travel. Share your plan with them and ask their advice on how to achieve your professional goals. Most people are more than eager to share their experience to help others avoid the pitfalls they may have faced in the past.

ASK FOR FEEDBACK

Even if you feel like you know yourself, it is always good to have another perspective. Sometimes we don't know how we come across to others in certain situations. Professionally, your boss or business partner should be giving you feedback. If they're not, ask them. You want to make sure you are meeting expectations. Ask people in your network, peers and direct-reports, if you have them. There is always room for improvement, so be open to the constructive criticism of those you respect.

TAKE ADVANTAGE OF TRAINING

Many companies offer voluntary, on the job training programs. Not only are trainings a way to get paid for learning something new, but they are great resume builders. Once you are trained on something, you can list it as part of your work experience if applicable. Additionally, you may go into a training session because it offers insight about a future job that you are considering. After completing it you may learn that task is not what you thought it was, and may or may not still be interested in it. If you are in business there are many free or low cost workshops for just about every situation and skill.

CONTINUALLY LEARN

Some companies don't offer voluntary training classes for your interests. Books, online classes and workshops can help fulfill your needs. Your professional development is your responsibility. It would be nice to get some help from your employer, but that's not always possible. Do some research and find out what is available to help you learn new things or get better at what you are already doing.

TREAT EVERYONE WITH RESPECT

This seems like a "no-brainer," but in my experience it is not always a given. Aside from the fact that it's professional and the right thing to do, depending on your job or business, it's a small world. Someone you disrespected as one of your employees may end up being your boss in a few years. A salesperson you abruptly blew off a few months ago may end up being the company representative for the account you are trying land.

PRACTICE HEALTHY COMPETITION

We are always "sizing up" others, especially if they are where we would like to be. There's nothing wrong with that. You should always know who you are up against. But don't use unethical or immoral tactics to get ahead of the competition. Whether it's manipulating the numbers, bad-mouthing someone or other forms of sabotage, none of it is necessary. Healthy competition should inspire you to work harder, not play dirty.

STAY ON THE HIGH ROAD

Just because everyone in the department is surfing the internet or talking on the phone doesn't mean you have to do it too. It may seem like they are getting away with it now, but there are always consequences for those actions. Besides, if you are trying to get ahead, those slackers are actually making it easier for you to rise above the crowd. If you are in business and you observe questionable activities, do not engage. You have a reputation to maintain and practicing risky behavior could ruin it.

BE A TRUE TEAM PLAYER

I specified "true" because there are times when people use the phrase "team player" when trying to convince you to do something ethically questionable. That is not what I am referring to. What I mean is at least pull your own weight and be willing to do more than your share to achieve the goal. In reality, not everyone on the team is going to have the same skill level as you. You have to be okay with that. If there is extra work to be done and you can handle it, just do it! The number one biggest career killer is the phrase, "That's not my job."

Hopefully this will get you off to a good start or further along in your journey if you have already begun. This list by no means covers all of *The Subtle Shark* career tips, but these are my top ten. I will continue to explore each of these topics and more on a deeper level in future books, workshops and blogs.

APPENDIX
SUBTLE SHARK TRAITS

Throughout this book I highlighted 20 traits of *The Subtle Shark.* Alone these qualities aren't anything new or fancy. I wanted to provide anecdotal support to show how they worked for me. Maybe various aspects will work for you. Some of these characteristics I exhibited instinctively and others I developed <u>after</u> certain experiences. Answering the accompanying questions may help you work through similar situations or explore what you will do differently going forward.

1-THE SUBTLE SHARK IS TRUSTWORTHY

In your career or your business, how do you build trust with others?

____

What personal values guide your professional interactions?

____

2-THE SUBTLE SHARK DOES NOT ACCEPT MEDIOCRITY

In what ways do you strive for excellence in your career or your business?

____

What personal characteristics of yourself and others do you consider "deal-breakers" in your professional interactions?

____

3-THE SUBTLE SHARK IS DETERMINED BUT WILLING TO COMPROMISE
In your career or your business, when is it best to compromise?

____

When have you felt like giving up, even on something you really need?

____

____

4-THE SUBTLE SHARK BELIEVES IN SHARED CONTRIBUTIONS
In your career or your business, are you only focused on your needs?

____

What is your definition of teamwork & how do you contribute?

____

____

5-THE SUBTLE SHARK BUILDS A SOLID REPUTATION
What have you done to build a name for yourself in your career or your business?

____

Do others know who you are and what they can expect from you?

____

____

6-THE SUBTLE SHARK ASKS FOR HELP AND ADAPTS TO CHANGE

What big changes are you experiencing in your career or your business?

____

____

Are you being honest with yourself about whether or not you need help?

____

____

7-THE SUBTLE SHARK LEARNS FROM MISTAKES AND TRIES AGAIN

What professional failures are you facing?

____

____

What is your plan to learn from them and start over?

____

____

8-THE SUBTLE SHARK GAINS EXPERIENCE THEN MOVES FORWARD

Your career or business may not yet be where you'd like right now, but what experience are you gaining that will help you get there?

____

____

What is your plan for getting to the next level?

____

____

9-THE SUBTLE SHARK LEARNS FROM GOOD AND BAD LEADERS
What positive traits are you learning from other professionals that will help your career or business?

____

____

What have you learned NOT to do?

____

____

10-THE SUBTLE SHARK PREPARES FOR THE NEXT OPPORTUNITY
What is the next step in your career or business?

____

____

How will you know when it is time to pursue that next step?

____

____

11-THE SUBTLE SHARK DOES NOT GET DISTRACTED BY NEGATIVITY
What outside influences are you allowing to distract you from your goals?

____

____

What do you need to do to regain focus?

____

____

12-THE SUBTLE SHARK REALIZES EVERY OPPORTUNITY IS NOT THE BEST ONE

What opportunities are you being offered that don't fit with your plan or your skill set?

____

____

What "good" opportunities have your realized are not good for you?

____

____

13-THE SUBTLE SHARK EMBRACES BEING A LEADER

What aspects of being a leader are you trying to suppress?

____

____

What past experiences derailed you from your true calling?

____

____

14-THE SUBTLE SHARK DOES NOT WORK IN A SILO

What type of relationships do you have with your colleagues?

____

____

How are you helping them to become better?

____

____

15-THE SUBTLE SHARK WORKS THROUGH ADVERSITY

What hardships are you currently experiencing in your career or business?

____

What are you doing to work through any setbacks that arise?

____

16-THE SUBTLE SHARK KEEPS MOVING FORWARD

Are you dwelling on past adversities or are you focused on the future?

____

How can you take all the experience you've gained so far and turn it into new opportunities?

____

17-THE SUBTLE SHARK SEES THE BIG PICTURE

What mundane details are occupying the majority of your time?

____

What is the long-term vision for your career or business?

____

18-THE SUBTLE SHARAK TAKES ON NEW CHALLENGES

What challenges have you shunned in order to stay in your comfort zone?

How quickly do you tackle new challenges so that you are ready for the next?

19- THE SUBTLE SHARK EXPANDS THE SPHERE OF INFLUENCE

Who is part of your professional network?

How do you provide value to their career or business & how do they do the same for you?

20- THE SUBTLE SHARK SHARES KNOWLEDGE

What are you doing to continue your professional development?

How are you helping others to improve their skills?

Learn more about:

Business Consulting Offerings
Workshops
Special Events
at
www.arpattersonconsulting.com
blog.ayesharpattersoncoaching.com

Learn more about:

Career Coaching Offerings
Workshops
Special Events
at
www.ayesharpattersoncoaching.com
blog.arpattersonconsulting.com

Follow Us:

www.twitter.com/AyeshaPatterson
www.facebook.com/AyeshaRPattersonConsulting

The Subtle Shark: Redefining Career Achievement

www.ingramcontent.com/pod-product-compliance
Lightning Source LLC
Chambersburg PA
CBHW061031050726
47592CB00004B/1395